CONTENTS

On the cover (left to right): Crunchy Apple-Cranberry Muffins, White Lace Inn; Tomato Curry Soup, Castle Marne; Steak with Herbed Butter, Windmill Inn; Smoked Chicken and Asparagus with Penne, The Roycroft Inn.

Note: At the beginning of each recipe, preparation times are noted. The Prep Time tells the active "hands on" preparation time. The Ready in minutes/hours indicates the time required, beyond the active "hands on" preparation, for baking, cooking, marinating, grilling, cooling, refrigerating or freezing.

Holiday Dinner

A selection of delicious recipes to enhance your holiday entertaining.

❄ ❄

The Red Lion Inn

Stockbridge, Massachusetts

*T*he historic Red Lion Inn is located in Stockbridge, Massachusetts. Originally built in 1773 as a welcome stop for coaches traveling between Albany, New York, and Boston, Massachusetts, the Inn is proudly one of the few in New England operating continuously since before 1800.

The Inn offers rooms with all the amenities of today, decorated in an atmosphere steeped in colonial charm and history. To this day, it has one of the largest collections of colonial china, pictures, and furniture in the country.

The Red Lion Inn offers both formal and informal dining. Whether you choose to dine in the casual Widow Bingham Tavern with its nightly entertainment, the beautiful impatiens-filled courtyard, or the formal dining room, you will be graciously served the finest in contemporary New England cuisine.

As a guest of the Red Lion Inn, you will experience gracious hospitality in an atmosphere drenched in over 200 years of history.

Apple-Cranberry Crisp

Yield: 8 to 10 servings   Prep Time: 30 minutes (Ready in 1 hour, 30 minutes)

1 cup old-fashioned rolled oats	½ cup (1 stick) butter, melted
1 cup all-purpose flour	3½ pounds (about 7 large) tart apples
1 cup firmly packed brown sugar	1 cup cranberries
¼ teaspoon baking soda	¾ cup sugar
¼ teaspoon baking powder	1½ teaspoons cinnamon
¼ teaspoon salt	

1. Preheat oven to 350°F. Butter bottom only, of 8-inch square (2-quart) glass baking dish.

2. In large bowl, combine rolled oats, flour, brown sugar, baking soda, baking powder and salt; mix well. Add melted butter; blend until all dry ingredients are moistened.

3. Peel, core and slice apples; place in another large bowl. Stir in cranberries. Add sugar and cinnamon; toss until well coated.

4. Place half of oat mixture in buttered baking dish; press in firmly. Pour apple-cranberry mixture over top. Cover with remaining oat mixture.

5. Bake at 350°F for 1 hour or until apples are tender.

NEW ENGLAND CLAM CHOWDER

Yield: 8 (1⅓-cup) servings   Prep Time: 50 minutes

4	cups warm water	¼	lb. salt pork,* cut into pieces
24	fresh clams in the shell	1	cup chopped onions
1	teaspoon salt	2	tablespoons all-purpose flour
¼	teaspoon white pepper	2	cups milk
¼	teaspoon Worcestershire sauce	1	cup light cream
2	cups diced peeled potatoes	1	tablespoon butter

1. In large saucepan, combine warm water, clams, salt, pepper and Worcestershire sauce. Bring to a boil. Boil 12 to 18 minutes or until clams open. Discard any clams that do not open.

2. Strain clams; reserve both clams and cooking broth. Remove meat from clam shells; mince clams. Set clams aside.

3. In medium saucepan, combine potatoes and 2 cups of clam broth; discard remaining broth. Bring to a boil. Reduce heat; gently simmer about 10 minutes or until potatoes are cooked but still firm. Drain.

4. Meanwhile, in same large saucepan, cook salt pork about 5 minutes. Remove salt pork from saucepan; set aside. Reserve 2 tablespoons drippings in saucepan.

5. Add onions to salt pork drippings; cook over medium heat for about 4 minutes or until tender. Stir in flour until well blended. Cook 5 to 6 minutes, stirring constantly.

6. Add 1 cup clam broth; cook until hot and smooth. Stir in milk, cream, potatoes, clams and salt pork. Cook until thoroughly heated; do not boil. Just before serving, stir in butter until melted.

TIP:
*¼ lb. bacon can be substituted for salt pork.

VEAL OSCAR WITH HOLLANDAISE SAUCE

Yield: 4 servings (¾ cup sauce)
Prep Time: 30 minutes

HOLLANDAISE SAUCE*

2 egg yolks
2 tablespoons fresh lemon juice
1 tablespoon cold water
½ cup butter (1 stick), softened, cut into pieces
½ teaspoon salt
⅛ teaspoon ground red pepper (cayenne)
¼ teaspoon Worcestershire sauce

VEAL OSCAR

¼ cup all-purpose flour
¼ teaspoon salt
⅛ teaspoon pepper
4 veal cutlets, pounded very thin
2 tablespoons butter
1 cup cooked lobster meat**
12 asparagus spears, cooked until crisp-tender

1. In small heavy saucepan, combine egg yolks, lemon juice and water; mix well. Cook over low heat for 2 to 4 minutes, beating constantly with wire whisk, until mixture is a light custard consistency. Remove from heat; beat about 1 minute.

2. Over low heat, slowly beat in softened butter pieces, a little at a time. Stir in salt, ground red pepper and Worcestershire sauce. Cover to keep warm.

3. In shallow dish, combine flour, salt and pepper. Coat veal cutlets with flour mixture.

4. In large skillet, melt butter over medium-high heat. Add veal; cook 2 minutes on each side. Place veal on serving platter or individual plates.

5. To serve, top veal with lobster meat and 3 asparagus spears. Spoon hollandaise sauce over asparagus. Serve immediately.

TIPS:
*Hollandaise sauce should be used immediately or refrigerated for 2 to 3 days.

**To cook lobster, bring enough salted water to cover lobster, to a boil. Add lobster; return to a boil. Reduce heat; cover and simmer about 8 minutes or until lobster turns bright red. Once cooled, remove meat from claws and tail.

VEAL SCALLOPS WITH MUSHROOMS, HAM AND CHEESE

Yield: 4 servings
Prep Time: 50 minutes

½ cup (1 stick) butter
4 tablespoons minced shallots
½ pound fresh mushrooms, sliced
2 cups heavy cream
4 (6-ounce) veal cutlets, pounded ¼-inch thick
½ teaspoon salt
¼ teaspoon pepper
2 tablespoons all-purpose flour
⅔ cup dry white wine
4 thin slices cooked ham, cut into small thin strips
4 thin slices Swiss cheese

1. In large skillet, melt ¼ cup of the butter. Add 2 tablespoons of the shallots; cook over medium heat for 2 to 3 minutes or until tender. Stir in mushrooms; cook about 10 minutes or until moisture has evaporated.

2. Stir in ⅔ cup of the cream. Cook about 10 minutes or until cream has been reduced by half and sauce has thickened considerably, stirring occasionally. Cover; keep warm over low heat.

3. Sprinkle veal with salt and pepper; coat with flour. Melt remaining ¼ cup butter in another skillet. Add cutlets; cook over medium heat for 2 minutes on each side or until no longer pink in center. Place in glass baking dish; cover to keep warm.

4. Pour off any butter remaining in skillet. Add remaining 2 tablespoons shallots and the wine. Cook over high heat about 4 minutes or until mixture is reduced by ⅓, stirring constantly.

5. Stir in remaining 1⅓ cups cream; cook about 10 minutes or until mixture is reduced by half and has thickened considerably. Season to taste with salt and pepper.

6. Top each cutlet with creamed mushrooms, ham, 1 cheese slice and sauce. Broil 4 to 6 inches from heat for 2 minutes. Serve immediately.

NEW YEAR'S EVE PARTY

Include these fabulous recipes when planning your New Year's Eve celebration.

❋ ❋

RABBIT HILL INN
Lower Waterford, Vermont

*T*he romantic Rabbit Hill Inn is located in the village of Lower Waterford, Vermont.

Tucked away amid the mountains and picturesque countryside, Rabbit Hill is a beautifully restored, classic New England Inn.

Originally built in 1795, the Inn provided lodging for weary traders and loggers.

Today, the Rabbit Hill Inn is a romantic hideaway dedicated to pampering its guests with individualized service. The guest rooms are all beautifully

appointed, creating an atmosphere of romance and comfort, complete with candlelight and soft music.

Attention to detail is carried through into the dining experience at the Rabbit Hill Inn. Meals are prepared with seasonal ingredients, creating the finest in contemporary cuisine, and served on beautiful crystal and fine china.

In the midst of the beautiful, unspoiled Vermont countryside, the Rabbit Hill Inn offers a sophisticated blend of liveliness with a peaceful step right out of time.

CHOCOLATE CRANBERRY PATÉ

Yield: 16 servings   Prep Time: 20 minutes (Ready in 8 hours, 20 minutes)

15 ounces bittersweet chocolate, chopped	4 egg yolks
1 cup heavy cream	1½ cups powdered sugar
4 tablespoons unsalted butter, cut into pieces	2 to 4 tablespoons dark rum
	½ cup halved cranberries

1. Line bottom and sides of 8x4-inch loaf pan with plastic wrap. In medium saucepan, combine chocolate, cream and butter; cook over low heat until mixture is melted and smooth, stirring occasionally.

2. With wire whisk, beat in egg yolks one at a time until well blended. Cook over low heat for 2 to 3 minutes. Beat in powdered sugar and rum. Gently stir in cranberries.

3. Pour hot mixture into plastic wrap-lined pan. Cover; refrigerate at least 8 hours or overnight.

4. To serve, invert paté onto large plate to unmold; remove plastic wrap. Cut into ½-inch slices.

APRICOT ANGEL SQUARES

Yield: 12 servings   Prep Time: 20 minutes (Ready in 1 hour, 20 minutes)

CRUST
- 2 cups all-purpose flour
- 2 tablespoons sugar
- ¼ teaspoon salt
- ½ cup (1 stick) butter, softened
- ¼ cup heavy cream

FILLING
- 1½ cups apricot preserves
- 2 tablespoons lemon juice

TOPPING
- 1½ cups firmly packed brown sugar
- 1 cup shredded coconut
- ½ cup chopped pecans
- ¼ cup all-purpose flour
- ½ teaspoon baking soda
- ½ cup light corn syrup
- ¼ cup (½ stick) butter, softened
- 4 eggs

1. Heat oven to 350°F. In medium bowl, combine all crust ingredients; mix until coarse crumbs form. Press in bottom of ungreased 13x9-inch pan. Bake at 350°F for 10 minutes. Cool.

2. Meanwhile, in small saucepan, combine preserves and lemon juice; heat over low heat, stirring until well blended. Set aside.

3. In large bowl, combine all topping ingredients; beat 3 to 4 minutes or until light and fluffy. Spread preserves mixture over baked crust. Pour and spread topping mixture evenly over preserves mixture.

4. Bake at 350°F for 40 to 45 minutes or until top is deep golden brown. Cool 15 minutes. Cut into squares; serve warm.

Blue Cheese Walnut Appetizer

Yield: 24 servings   Prep Time: 30 minutes
(Ready in 2 hours, 20 minutes)

1   cup dry bread crumbs
½   cup finely chopped walnuts, toasted*
3   tablespoons butter, melted
1   pound blue cheese, crumbled
1   (8-ounce) package cream cheese, softened
4   eggs, beaten

Assorted crackers

1. Heat oven to 325°F. Butter bottom only of 10-inch springform pan; line bottom with waxed paper.

2. In small bowl, combine bread crumbs, walnuts and butter; mix well. Press in bottom of buttered pan lined with waxed-paper.

3. In large bowl, beat blue cheese and cream cheese until well blended. With mixer running, add eggs one at a time, beating well after each addition until smooth. Pour mixture over crust.

4. Bake at 325°F for 45 to 50 minutes or until knife inserted in center comes out clean.

5. Cool in pan on wire rack for 1 hour. Run knife around edge of pan; remove sides of pan. Cool slightly and serve warm, or refrigerate 8 hours or until serving time.

6. Just before serving, invert onto serving plate. Cut into wedges or serve with assorted crackers.

TIP:
*To toast walnuts, spread on cookie sheet; bake at 350°F for 5 to 7 minutes or until golden brown, stirring occasionally.

Jalapeño Cheddar Appetizer Pie

Yield: 24 servings   Prep Time: 25 minutes
(Ready in 2 hours, 25 minutes)

CRUST
1   cup dry bread crumbs
¼   cup grated Parmesan cheese
¼   cup (½ stick) butter, melted

FILLING
4   (8-ounce) packages cream cheese, softened
⅓   cup beer, if desired
5   whole eggs
3   egg yolks
¼   cup all-purpose flour
3   cups (12 ounces) finely shredded Cheddar cheese
½   cup finely chopped onion
2   tablespoons chopped fresh herbs (such as basil, thyme, chives, parsley and/or cilantro)
2   jalapeño peppers, minced
1   garlic clove, minced

1. Heat oven to 350°F. Lightly butter 10-inch springform pan. In small bowl, combine all crust ingredients; mix well. Press in bottom of buttered pan.

2. In large bowl, combine cream cheese, beer, whole eggs, egg yolks and flour; beat until well blended. In medium bowl, combine cheese, onion, herbs, peppers and garlic; mix well. Add to cream cheese mixture; mix until well blended. Pour over crust in pan.

3. Bake at 350°F for 1 hour or until knife inserted in center comes out clean. Cool in pan on wire rack for 1 hour. Run knife around edge of pan; remove sides of pan. Serve warm or refrigerate until serving time.

Shelled nuts remain fresh
for several months if
stored tightly covered
in the refrigerator or freezer.

Store leavening agents
such as baking soda and
baking powder
in a cool, dry place.

GAME DAY

❋ ❋

*N*o question that those special football games of the season lure family and friends to the TV set. It's party time, and you need hearty fare for your armchair sports fans! Get them started with our "Great Ball of Fire," a tasty ham and cheese spread. Next, guests can tackle Easy Cheesy Bean Dip that can be as fiery as you choose. Buttery Party Snack Mix is also a crowd pleaser. Spicy Honey Chicken Drumettes and/or Easy Southern-Style Ribs can be served up as a second course, hot from the oven. If you'd like, guests can help assemble Chicken and Black Bean Tostizzas, as easy to eat as individual pizzas. When the game is over, hot, steamy coffee and Salted Peanut Chews will score big points!

EASY SOUTHERN-STYLE RIBS

Yield: 5 servings   Prep Time: 10 minutes
(Ready in 1 hour, 55 minutes)

SPICE RUB

1½   teaspoons salt
1½   teaspoons Ac´cent® Flavor Enhancer
1   teaspoon chili powder
½   teaspoon pepper
3½   to 4 lb. pork spareribs, cut into 6-inch sections

SAUCE

1½   cups barbecue sauce
2   teaspoons chili powder
½   teaspoon Ac´cent® Flavor Enhancer
½   teaspoon hot pepper sauce
2   garlic cloves, minced

1. Heat oven to 325°F. Line 15x10x1-inch baking pan with foil; place wire rack in pan.

2. In small bowl, combine all spice rub ingredients except ribs; blend well. Place ribs on rack in pan, meaty side up. Rub spice mixture over both sides of ribs, pressing lightly. Bake at 325°F for 45 minutes.

3. In small bowl, combine all sauce ingredients; mix well. Brush ribs with sauce. Bake an additional 40 to 60 minutes or until ribs are tender, brushing frequently with sauce.

GRILLING DIRECTIONS:
1. Heat grill. Prepare and rub spice mixture on ribs as directed above. Place ribs on gas grill over medium-low heat or on charcoal grill 6 to 8 inches from medium coals. Cover; cook 45 minutes.

2. Prepare sauce as directed above. Brush ribs with sauce. Cook an additional 40 to 60 minutes or until ribs are tender, turning and brushing frequently with sauce.

SALTED PEANUT CHEWS

Yield: 36 bars   Prep Time: 40 minutes
(Ready in 1 hour, 40 minutes)

BASE

1   pkg. Pillsbury Moist Supreme® Yellow Cake Mix
⅓   cup (⅔ stick) butter, softened
1   egg
3   cups miniature marshmallows

TOPPING

⅔   cup corn syrup
¼   cup (½ stick) butter
2   teaspoons vanilla
1   (10-oz.) pkg. peanut butter chips
2   cups crisp rice cereal
2   cups salted peanuts

1. Heat oven to 350°F. In large bowl, combine cake mix, ⅓ cup butter and egg at low speed until crumbly. Press in bottom of ungreased 13x9-inch pan.

2. Bake at 350°F for 12 to 18 minutes or until light golden brown. Remove from oven; immediately sprinkle with marshmallows. Return to oven; bake an additional 1 to 2 minutes or until marshmallows just begin to puff. Cool while preparing topping.

3. In large saucepan, combine all topping ingredients except cereal and peanuts. Heat just until chips are melted and mixture is smooth, stirring constantly. Remove from heat; stir in cereal and peanuts. Immediately spoon warm topping over marshmallows; spread to cover. Refrigerate 1 hour or until firm. Cut into bars. Store in covered container.

GREAT BALL OF FIRE

Yield: 2 cups   Prep Time: 15 minutes (Ready in 2 hours, 45 minutes)

1 (4¼-oz.) can Underwood® Deviled Ham Spread

1 (3-oz.) pkg. cream cheese, softened

4 oz. (1 cup) shredded Cheddar cheese

3 tablespoons Old El Paso® Chopped Green Chiles

2 tablespoons finely chopped green onions, if desired

⅓ cup chopped walnuts

1. In small bowl, combine ham spread, cream cheese, Cheddar cheese, chiles and onions; mix well.

2. Shape mixture into ball. Roll in walnuts. Wrap in plastic wrap; refrigerate 2 hours.

3. Let ball stand at room temperature for 30 minutes to soften slightly before serving. Serve with crackers.

CHICKEN AND BLACK BEAN TOSTIZZAS

Yield: 8 mini-pizzas   Prep Time: 30 minutes (Ready in 55 minutes)

PIZZA
- 1 *(17.3-oz.) can Pillsbury Grands!® Refrigerated Buttermilk or Flaky Biscuits*
- 1 *cup diced cooked chicken*
- 1 *cup canned Green Giant®, Joan of Arc® or Progresso® Black Beans (from 15-oz. can), drained*
- ½ *cup Old El Paso® Salsa*
- ¼ *cup chopped fresh cilantro*
- ¼ *teaspoon cumin*
- 2 *green onions, chopped*
- ½ *cup green or red bell pepper strips (1 inch long)*
- 6 *oz. (1½ cups) shredded Cheddar cheese*

GARNISH, IF DESIRED
- ½ *cup sour cream*
- ½ *cup guacamole*

1. Heat oven to 350°F. Separate dough into 8 biscuits. On ungreased cookie sheets, press or roll each biscuit into 5½-inch round.

2. In medium bowl, combine chicken, beans, salsa, cilantro and cumin; mix well. Spread evenly over biscuits to within ¼ inch of edges. Top evenly with onions, bell pepper and cheese.

3. Bake at 350°F for 20 to 24 minutes or until biscuits are golden brown and cheese is melted. To serve, top with sour cream and guacamole.

EASY CHEESY BEAN DIP

Yield: 2¼ cups   Prep Time: 15 minutes

¼ cup Old El Paso® Salsa

1 (8-oz.) can bean dip

1 (4.5-oz.) can Old El Paso® Chopped Green Chiles, drained

8 oz. (2 cups) shredded American cheese

1. In medium saucepan, combine all ingredients; mix well. Cook over low heat for 8 to 10 minutes or until cheese is melted, stirring constantly.

2. Serve warm with tortilla chips.

MICROWAVE DIRECTIONS:
1. In 1½-quart microwave-safe bowl, combine salsa, bean dip and chiles; mix well. Microwave on HIGH for 4 to 4½ minutes or until mixture is hot, stirring once halfway through cooking.

2. Stir in cheese. Microwave on HIGH for 1 minute or until cheese is melted. Stir before serving with tortilla chips.

The marinade for the Spicy Honey Chicken Drumettes can be made ahead. Heavy-duty resealable plastic bags work well for marinating. They take less refrigerator space and can be turned as a unit to coat individual pieces.

PARTY SNACK MIX

Yield: 12 cups   Prep Time: 10 minutes
(Ready in 40 minutes)

4 cups bite-sized crispy corn squares cereal

2 cups bite-sized crispy wheat squares cereal

2 cups pretzel sticks

2 cups Spanish peanuts or mixed nuts

½ cup (1 stick) butter, melted

1 tablespoon Worcestershire sauce

⅛ teaspoon hot pepper sauce

1 teaspoon salt

¼ teaspoon garlic powder

1. Heat oven to 325°F. In large bowl, combine cereals, pretzel sticks and peanuts.

2. In small bowl, combine butter, Worcestershire sauce, hot pepper sauce, salt and garlic powder. Pour seasoning mixture over cereal mixture; toss to coat. Spread in ungreased 15x10x1-inch baking pan.

3. Bake at 325°F for 25 to 30 minutes or until lightly toasted, stirring occasionally.

SPICY HONEY CHICKEN DRUMETTES

Yield: 12 servings   Prep Time: 10 minutes
(Ready in 2 hours, 10 minutes)

¼ cup honey

¼ cup soy sauce

¼ cup chili sauce

¼ teaspoon ginger

¼ teaspoon dry mustard

½ teaspoon hot pepper sauce

12 chicken drumettes

1. In 12x8-inch (2-quart) baking dish, combine honey, soy sauce, chili sauce, ginger, dry mustard and hot pepper sauce; mix well. Add drumettes; turn to coat. Cover; refrigerate 1 hour to marinate.

2. Heat oven to 375°F. Uncover dish. Bake chicken in marinade at 375°F for 45 to 60 minutes or until chicken is tender and no longer pink next to bone, brushing with marinade occasionally.

WINTER SUPPER

Delicious and hearty recipes for the perfect winter meal.

❄ ❄

THE ROYCROFT INN

East Aurora, New York

The Roycroft Inn is located in the historic town of East Aurora, New York.

The Roycroft Inn was originally the dining and lodging facility as well as the social center of the Roycroft Community. Established in 1895 by Albert Hubbard, the community was centered on the philosophy of the Arts and Crafts movement. The spirit of the Arts and Crafts movement emphasized hand-crafted workmanship, strong sense of community, and a commitment to simple living.

Today, The Roycroft Inn features 22 first class guest rooms, three outstanding dining rooms and a relaxing lounge with fireplace and picturesque country garden. While preserving the past, the Inn offers all the amenities of modern day comfort.

The menu offered at Roycroft can be described as classic American cuisine. Only the freshest ingredients, including herbs picked from their own herb garden, are used in the preparation of each meal.

The unique history and beautiful surroundings of The Roycroft Inn create a memorable stay for its guests.

BISCOTTI

Yield: About 5 dozen biscotti   Prep Time: 20 minutes (Ready in 1 hour, 15 minutes)

6 eggs	1 cup (2 sticks) butter, melted
6 cups all-purpose flour	2 teaspoons orange extract
1 cup sugar	1 egg white, beaten
2 teaspoons baking powder	

1. Heat oven to 350°F. In small bowl, beat eggs; set aside.

2. In large bowl, combine flour, sugar and baking powder; mix well. Make a well in the center of flour mixture. Add butter, extract and eggs; mix until thoroughly blended and smooth.

3. Divide dough into four pieces. Press each piece into 10x3-inch rectangle. Place two rectangles on each of two ungreased cookie sheets. Brush each rectangle with beaten egg white.

4. Bake at 350°F for 15 to 20 minutes or until lightly browned. Cool on cookie sheets for 15 minutes.

5. Cut each rectangle into ½-inch thick slices. Place each slice, cut side down, on same cookie sheets.

6. Bake at 350°F for an additional 15 to 20 minutes or until crisp. Cool on wire racks.

SMOKED CHICKEN AND ASPARAGUS WITH PENNE

Yield: 4 (1½-cup) servings   Prep Time: 45 minutes

2   teaspoons water
½   teaspoon liquid smoke
2   (8-ounce) boneless chicken breasts
4   oz. (1½ cups) uncooked penne
    (tube-shaped pasta)
3   tablespoons butter
½   cup sliced leeks
1   garlic clove, minced
1   cup asparagus pieces
    (1½ inches), cooked

½   cup chopped roasted red bell peppers
    (from 7.25-ounce jar)
1   cup heavy cream
½   cup (2 ounces) finely shredded
    Romano cheese
¼   teaspoon salt
⅛   teaspoon pepper
¼   cup (1 ounce) crumbled Feta cheese

1. In small bowl, combine water and liquid smoke. Place chicken in large resealable food storage plastic bag; add liquid smoke mixture. Seal bag; turn bag gently to coat. Let stand at room temperature for 10 minutes, turning bag occasionally.

2. Place chicken on broiler pan. Broil 3 inches from heat, turning once, for 12 to 14 minutes or until chicken is fork-tender and juices run clear. Cool slightly; cut chicken into strips.

3. Meanwhile, cook penne to desired doneness as directed on package. Drain; cover to keep warm.

4. In large skillet, melt butter over medium-high heat. Add leeks and garlic; cook 2 to 3 minutes or until tender. Stir in chicken, asparagus and roasted red bell pepper. Cook 3 to 4 minutes or until thoroughly heated. Add cream; cook over medium-high heat for about 10 minutes or until cream reduces slightly.

5. Add cooked penne, Romano cheese, salt and pepper; toss gently. Sprinkle with Feta cheese.

BUTTERNUT SQUASH SOUP

Yield: 8 (1-cup) servings
Prep Time: 1 hour, 45 minutes

SPICED PUMPKIN SEEDS

- 1 cup pumpkin seeds
- 1 teaspoon salt
- 1 teaspoon nutmeg
- 1 teaspoon cinnamon
- 2 tablespoons butter, melted

SWEET POTATO CRISPS

- 4 cups vegetable oil
- 1 sweet potato, peeled, cut into very thin slices

SOUP

- ½ cup (1 stick) butter
- 2 (1-pound) small butternut squash, peeled, seeded and cut into ½-inch cubes
- 2 quarts (8 cups) milk
- 1 teaspoon nutmeg
- 1 teaspoon allspice
- ½ teaspoon salt
- ¼ teaspoon pepper
- 1 cup heavy cream

1. Heat oven to 300°F. In small bowl, combine all ingredients for spiced pumpkin seeds, mix well. Spread evenly on ungreased cookie sheet. Bake at 300°F for 45 minutes or until golden brown.

2. Meanwhile, melt ½ cup butter in 6-quart Dutch oven or stockpot. Add squash; cook until lightly browned.

3. Stir in milk, 1 teaspoon nutmeg, allspice, ½ teaspoon salt and pepper. Cover; simmer about 25 minutes or until squash is very tender.

4. Meanwhile, in deep fat fryer or large heavy saucepan, bring vegetable oil to 300°F. Fry sweet potato slices in hot oil until crisp. Drain on paper towels.

5. In food processor bowl with metal blade, puree squash mixture until smooth. Return to Dutch oven. Stir in cream; cook until thoroughly heated. Serve soup garnished with pumpkin seeds and sweet potato crisps.

Butter Equivalents

1 pound	=	4 sticks
	=	2 cups
	=	32 tablespoons
½ pound	=	2 sticks
	=	1 cup
	=	16 tablespoons
¼ pound	=	1 stick
	=	½ cup
	=	8 tablespoons
⅛ pound	=	½ stick
	=	¼ cup
	=	4 tablespoons

Softening Butter

When a recipe calls for softened butter, the butter should be soft enough to blend smoothly with other ingredients.

Room Temperature Softening:
Allow butter to stand at room temperature for 1 to 2 hours or until softened. To speed up this process, cut the butter into pieces first.

Quick Softening:
Cut butter into small pieces and beat with an electric mixer.

Microwave:
Microwave one stick (unwrapped) at a time on the lowest power setting, checking after 15 to 20 seconds. If the butter is inadvertently melted, save it for another use, as melted butter is not suitable for baking purposes unless specified.

LITE AND EASY ENTREES

❄ ❄ ❄ ❄ ❄ ❄ ❄ ❄ ❄ ❄ ❄ ❄ ❄ ❄ ❄ ❄ ❄ ❄ ❄

*T*hese quick and easy entrees are so delicious and hearty that you will enjoy them any night of the week, even when schedules are hectic. Turkey Tetrazzini, a one-pot dinner, is ready in 20 minutes. Just a few ingredients are needed to make a zesty chili or jambalaya. Herbed Fish and Vegetables bake in the oven just long enough for you to make a simple salad and set the table. Bon Appetit!

BAYOU SAUSAGE JAMBALAYA

Yield: 4 (1½-cup) servings
Prep Time: 30 minutes

½	lb. turkey kielbasa link sausage, cut into ½-inch-thick slices	1	(16-oz.) jar Old El Paso® Salsa
2	boneless skinless chicken breast halves, cut into bite-sized pieces	1½	cups uncooked instant white rice
		1	cup water
			Hot pepper sauce, if desired

1. Spray nonstick Dutch oven with nonstick cooking spray. Heat over medium-high heat until hot. Add sausage and chicken; cook and stir 5 to 8 minutes or until chicken is no longer pink.

2. Add salsa, rice and water; stir well. Bring to a boil. Reduce heat; cover and simmer 5 to 10 minutes or until rice is tender. If desired, add salt and pepper to taste. Serve with hot pepper sauce.

❄ ❄ ❄ ❄ ❄ ❄ ❄ ❄

Fin fish are grouped in families
that have similar
flavors, colors and textures
that can be prepared in the
same way. If a recipe calls for
a fish that is not available,
you can substitute
one from the same group.

❄ ❄ ❄ ❄ ❄ ❄ ❄ ❄

HERBED FISH AND VEGETABLES

Yield: 4 servings   Prep Time: 30 minutes

4	(4-oz.) flounder, sole or orange roughy fillets	12	very thin lime slices, if desired
1	tablespoon chopped fresh thyme or ½ teaspoon dried thyme leaves, crushed	1	(1-lb.) pkg. Green Giant Select® Frozen Broccoli, Carrots and Cauliflower, thawed
8	teaspoons chopped fresh chives or green onion tops	2	teaspoons butter

1. Heat oven to 400°F. Dry flounder fillets with paper towels. Place each fillet in center of 18x12-inch piece of foil. Sprinkle each with thyme and chives; top with lime slices.

2. Spoon vegetables next to each fish fillet. Top each with ½ teaspoon butter. Bring foil up over fish and vegetables, sealing securely with double-fold seals on top and sides to form packets. Place on 1 large or 2 small cookie sheets.

3. Bake at 400°F for 15 to 20 minutes or until fish flakes easily with fork and vegetables are thoroughly heated.

TURKEY TETRAZZINI

Yield: 4 (1-cup) servings   Prep Time: 20 minutes

1   *(1-lb.) pkg. Green Giant® Pasta Accents® Primavera Frozen Vegetables with Pasta*
½   *lb. cooked turkey breast, cut into ½-inch cubes*

¾   *cup skim milk*
6   *fresh medium basil leaves, thinly sliced, or ½ teaspoon dried basil leaves*
¼   *cup grated Parmesan cheese*

1. In medium saucepan, combine all ingredients except cheese. Bring to a boil.

2. Cover; cook over medium heat for 6 to 8 minutes or until vegetables are crisp-tender, stirring occasionally.

3. Stir in Parmesan cheese.

THICK AND HEARTY VEGETABLE CHILI

Yield: 4 (1½-cup) servings   Prep Time: 25 minutes

2   *(14.5-oz.) cans chili-style chunky tomatoes, undrained*
1   *(15-oz.) can Green Giant® or Joan of Arc® Garbanzo Beans or Progresso® Chick Peas, drained, rinsed*
1   *(15-oz.) can Green Giant®, Joan of Arc® or Progresso® Black Beans, drained, rinsed*

1½   *cups Green Giant® Niblets® Frozen Corn*
2   *to 3 teaspoons chili powder*

1. In large saucepan, combine all ingredients; mix well. Bring to a boil over medium-high heat. Reduce heat; cover and simmer about 10 minutes to blend flavors.

2. To serve, ladle chili into 4 individual soup bowls. If desired, top with light sour cream.

VALENTINE'S DAY CELEBRATION

Delicious recipes "to fall in love with" on Valentine's Day.

❄ ❄

ROSE INN

Ithaca, New York

*T*he Rose Inn is located in Ithaca, New York. The large and classic Italianate mansion was originally built on 20 acres in 1842 as a private home. In 1983 the house was purchased and graciously restored into what is now known as the Rose Inn.

The magnificent architectural details of the mansion, combined with the beautiful surroundings provide guests with four star accommodations. Rooms are individually and luxuriously decorated. The formal parlor is a charming gathering place for Inn guests who enjoy a fine library and good company.

In the various dining rooms, guests enjoy a full country breakfast including homemade jams and preserves as well as memorable gourmet dinners.

Many of the Inn's favorite recipes are prepared with ingredients grown on the property. The apple orchard has 15 varieties of apple trees providing delicious homemade cider.

The Rose Inn has greatly succeeded in offering its guests beautiful accommodations and a first class dining experience.

HERB RICE

Yield: 6 servings   Prep Time: 15 minutes (Ready in 1 hour)

1   *cup uncooked converted rice*

1   *small onion, chopped (¼ cup)*

1   *cup button mushrooms, fresh preferred*

¼   *cup (½ stick) butter*

2   *tablespoons chopped mixed fresh Italian herbs (such as basil and oregano)*

2   *teaspoons beef-flavor instant bouillon*

¼   *teaspoon salt*

2   *cups water*

1. Heat oven to 350°F. Place rice in ungreased 1½-quart casserole. Add onion, mushrooms, butter, herbs, bouillon, salt and water; mix well.

2. Bake at 350°F for 45 minutes or until all liquid has been absorbed and top is brown. Stir before serving.

SALMON FILLETS WITH PINK GRAPEFRUIT BEURRE BLANC

Yield: 4 servings   Prep Time: 35 minutes

GASTRIQUE (Grapefruit Syrup)
- ¼ cup sugar
- 1 tablespoon white wine
- ½ cup fresh pink grapefruit juice or canned unsweetened grapefruit juice

SAUCE
- 2 shallots, minced (2 tablespoons)
- ¾ cup white wine
- ¼ cup white wine vinegar
- ½ cup heavy cream

- 1 cup (2 sticks) unsalted butter, cut into small pieces, softened
- Salt to taste

GRILL
- 4 fresh salmon fillets
- 2 tablespoons butter, melted
- ¼ teaspoon salt
- ⅛ teaspoon pepper
- 2 cups fresh spinach, wilted, warm

1. In small heavy saucepan, combine sugar and 1 tablespoon wine. Cook over high heat for about 3 minutes; do not stir. When light brown caramel stage is reached, slowly add grapefruit juice, stirring constantly. Cook about 5 minutes until reduced by half, stirring occasionally until syrup lightly coats spoon. Remove from heat; set aside.

2. In large skillet, combine shallots, ¾ cup wine and vinegar; cook over medium-high heat for 8 to 10 minutes or until one tablespoon liquid remains.

3. Add cream; cook about 5 minutes or until mixture thickly coats spoon. Strain mixture; return to skillet. Bring to a boil; remove from heat. Add butter gradually, stirring constantly. Add salt to taste. Stir in gastrique; keep warm, but not hot.

4. Brush salmon fillets with melted butter; sprinkle with salt and pepper. Place on gas or charcoal grill; cook 10 to 12 minutes, turning once, or until fish flakes easily with fork. Carefully turn salmon over; peel skin from bottom of each fillet.

5. To serve, place wilted spinach on 4 individual dinner plates. Place salmon fillets over spinach; spoon sauce over salmon.

MONT BLANC

Yield: 6 servings
Prep Time: 1 hour (Ready in 2 hours)

MERINGUE SHELLS
4   egg whites
½   teaspoon cream of tartar
1   cup sugar

CHANTILLY CREAM
1½ cups heavy cream
½   cup sugar
1   teaspoon vanilla

CHESTNUT PURÉE MOUSSE
¾   cup chestnut purée (from 16-ounce can)
½   cup firmly packed brown sugar
½   teaspoon vanilla

RASPBERRY PURÉE
1   pint (2 cups) fresh raspberries, reserving 18 berries for garnish

1. Heat oven to 275°F. Line cookie sheet with parchment paper or foil. In large bowl, beat egg whites and cream of tartar at medium speed until soft peaks form. Add 1 cup sugar, 2 tablespoons at a time, beating at high speed for about 10 minutes or until stiff glossy peaks form and sugar is almost dissolved.

2. Fill large decorating bag with large star tip. Fill bag with meringue; pipe six 3-inch diameter hearts onto paper-lined cookie sheet. With remaining meringue fill in center of each heart.

3. Bake at 275°F for 35 minutes or until lightly browned around edges. For softer meringues, remove cookie sheet from oven immediately and cool on wire rack. For dry, crisp meringues, turn oven off and leave meringues in oven with door closed for at least 2 hours or overnight.

4. Meanwhile, in small bowl, combine cream, ½ cup sugar and 1 teaspoon vanilla; beat until soft peaks form. Set aside.

5. In medium bowl, combine chestnut purée, brown sugar and ½ teaspoon vanilla; blend well. Fold in ⅔ cup chantilly cream. Refrigerate 1 hour.

6. Place raspberries in food processor bowl with metal blade; process until smooth. Strain to remove seeds.

7. To serve, carefully remove meringues from paper; place on individual dessert plates. Spoon chestnut purée mousse into center of each meringue. Top with a dollop of chantilly cream, 2 tablespoons raspberry purée and reserved fresh raspberries.

OPEN APPLE TART

Yield: 8 servings
Prep Time: 30 minutes (Ready in 55 minutes)

1   refrigerated pie crust (from 15-ounce package)
¼   cup (½ stick) butter
3   tart apples, peeled, sliced
4   tablespoons brown sugar
4   tablespoons apricot preserves or orange marmalade
Zest of 1 lemon
½   cup sour cream
1   egg
2   teaspoons all-purpose flour
¼   teaspoon cinnamon
1   tablespoon dark rum
½   teaspoon vanilla
½   cup coconut
½   cup chopped pecans

1. Heat oven to 450°F. Prepare pie crust as directed on package for one-crust baked shell using 10-inch tart pan with removable bottom. Bake at 450°F for 9 to 11 minutes or until light golden brown. Cool completely. Reduce oven temperature to 375°F.

2. In large skillet, melt butter. Add apples and 2 tablespoons of the brown sugar; cover and cook about 10 minutes, stirring occasionally.

3. Add 2 tablespoons of the preserves and the lemon zest. Increase heat; cook, uncovered, about 10 minutes or until almost dry.

4. Meanwhile, spread remaining 2 tablespoons preserves in bottom of cooled baked shell.

5. In small bowl, combine sour cream, egg, flour, cinnamon, rum, vanilla and remaining 2 tablespoons brown sugar; blend well. Add to apple mixture in skillet; mix well. Spoon into baked shell. Sprinkle with coconut and pecans.

6. Bake at 375°F for 20 to 25 minutes or until lightly browned. Serve warm.

❄ ❄ ❄ ❄ ❄ ❄ ❄ ❄

When grating lemon, lime or orange, use only the colored part of the rind. The inner white part is bitter.

❄ ❄ ❄ ❄ ❄ ❄ ❄ ❄

QUICK ONE-DISH MEALS

❄ ❄

*H*aving time is on just about everyone's agenda and having time-saving ingredients on hand for making family meals can help. These easy-to-make one-dish recipes take advantage of convenience products readily available in your supermarket deli, refrigerated and frozen food sections and grocery shelves. Add a crisp green salad, a warm dinner bread and beverage of your choice for three delicious, satisfying meals.

BROCCOLI BASIL LASAGNA ROLLS

Yield: 6 servings
Prep Time: 35 minutes

6   uncooked lasagna noodles
1   (9-oz.) pkg. Green Giant® Harvest Fresh® Frozen Cut Broccoli, thawed, well drained and chopped
1   cup Ricotta cheese
¼   cup grated Parmesan cheese

1   tablespoon chopped fresh basil or 1 teaspoon dried basil leaves
1   (14-oz.) jar spaghetti sauce
4   oz. (1 cup) shredded Mozzarella cheese

1. Cook noodles to desired doneness as directed on package. Drain; rinse with cold water.

2. Meanwhile, in medium bowl, combine broccoli, Ricotta cheese, Parmesan cheese and basil; mix well. Place lasagna noodles on work surface; spread about ⅓ cup broccoli mixture over each noodle. Roll up noodles; place seam side down on microwave-safe plate or in container. Microwave immediately, or cover and refrigerate to be used within 3 days.

3. To prepare each serving, place 1 lasagna roll on microwave-safe plate. Spoon ¼ cup spaghetti sauce over roll; top with 2 heaping tablespoons Mozzarella cheese. Cover with microwave-safe plastic wrap.

4. Microwave on HIGH for 1½ to 2½ minutes or until hot. Repeat for remaining lasagna rolls.

DIJON FETTUCCINE WITH TUNA

Yield: 4 (1¼-cup) servings
Prep Time: 40 minutes

1   (9-oz.) pkg. refrigerated fettuccine
1   tablespoon butter
1   tablespoon Pillsbury BEST® or Martha White® All Purpose Flour
¼   teaspoon salt
⅛   teaspoon pepper
1   cup half-and-half

1   tablespoon Dijon mustard
2   cups Green Giant® Frozen Cut Leaf Spinach
1   (12-oz.) can water-packed tuna, drained
1   (2-oz.) jar sliced pimientos, drained

1. In large saucepan, cook fettuccine to desired doneness as directed on package. Drain; rinse with hot water. Cover to keep warm.

2. In same saucepan, melt butter over medium heat. Stir in flour, salt and pepper. Cook until mixture is smooth and bubbly, stirring constantly. Gradually add half-and-half and mustard. Cook until mixture boils and thickens, stirring constantly.

3. Reduce heat to low; stir in spinach, tuna, pimientos and fettuccine. Cook over low heat for about 5 minutes or until thoroughly heated, stirring occasionally.

QUICK CHICKEN DIVAN

Yield: 5 servings   Prep Time: 10 minutes
(Ready in 45 minutes)

1   (1-lb.) pkg. Green Giant® Frozen
     Broccoli Cuts

2   cups cubed cooked chicken

1   (10¾-oz.) can
     condensed cream of chicken soup

½   cup reduced-calorie mayonnaise or
     salad dressing

1   teaspoon lemon juice

2   oz. (½ cup) shredded Cheddar cheese

¾   cup Progresso® Plain Bread Crumbs

2   tablespoons butter, melted

1. Heat oven to 350°F. Butter 12x8-inch (2-quart) baking dish.

2. Cook broccoli as directed on package; drain. Arrange broccoli in greased baking dish. Layer chicken over broccoli.

3. In small bowl, combine soup, mayonnaise and lemon juice; mix well. Spread over chicken; sprinkle with cheese. In another small bowl, combine bread crumbs and butter; sprinkle over top.

4. Bake at 350°F for 30 to 35 minutes or until thoroughly heated.

SOUTHERN SPECIALTIES

A delightful selection of southern recipes to welcome spring.

BRAND HOUSE AT ROSE HILL

Lexington, Kentucky

*T*he historic Brand House at Rose Hill is located in Lexington, Kentucky.

This gracious Southern inn was built by John Brand in 1812 as his private residence and lovingly named "Rose Hill."

Located in the heart of the bluegrass horse country, "Rose Hill" remained a private residence until 1995, when it opened its doors as a beautiful bed and breakfast and renamed "Brand House at Rose Hill."

Meticulously restored to retain its original ambiance, the inn provides all the contemporary convenience of comfortable elegance.

Each of the five rooms, some with fireplaces, have been professionally decorated in its own theme.

The inn serves a gourmet casual but elegant candle-lit breakfast in its grand dining room, complete with 13-foot ceilings and a 16-foot mahogany table set with linens, crystal, and china.

The Brand House at Rose Hill prides itself on offering its guests the finest in Southern hospitality with a unique flair.

SUGARED PECANS

Yield: 4½ cups   Prep Time: 15 minutes
(Ready in 50 minutes)

½	cup (1 stick) butter	1	cup sugar
2	egg whites	1	pound pecan halves

1. Heat oven to 325°F. Place butter in 15x10x1-inch baking pan; melt in oven for 2 to 3 minutes.

2. In small bowl, beat egg whites until stiff. Add sugar; beat well. Stir in pecans until covered with mixture. Pour mixture into baking pan; stir into melted butter.

3. Bake at 325°F for 30 to 35 minutes, stirring every 10 minutes. Spread on waxed paper; cool. Store in airtight container.

EASTER TREATS

*B*runch is often a convenient meal to prepare for an Easter family get-together and these recipes offer choices for easy accompaniments. Yummy Bunny Cake is the perfect centerpiece and dessert. It features the soft pastels of springtime and this charming fellow can add a touch of whimsy to the table setting. Everyone loves cinnamon and Cinnamon Pull Apart loaf is a fun way to serve it. Sour Cream Pound Cake and Strawberries and Cream Pie are two recipe classics that are certain to bring rave reviews.

YUMMY BUNNY CAKE

Yield: 12 servings   Prep Time: 25 minutes
(Ready in 2 hours, 5 minutes)

1   pkg. Pillsbury Moist Supreme® Cake Mix, any flavor
2   cans Pillsbury Creamy Supreme® Vanilla Frosting
1   (14-oz.) pkg. coconut

Food color
Pastel candy-coated chocolate pieces or chocolate chips
Jelly beans
Red string licorice

1. Butter and flour two 8 or 9-inch round cake pans as directed on package. Prepare and bake cake mix as directed on package. Cool 45 minutes or until completely cooled.

2. Cut cake as shown in diagrams. Frost sides of each cake piece. Assemble pieces on cookie sheet, large tray or 18x15-inch cardboard covered with foil as shown in diagrams. Frost top of cake. Sprinkle about 2⅔ cups coconut evenly over top and sides of cake, gently pressing coconut onto sides.

3. In small bowl, toss ¾ cup coconut with 2 to 3 drops red food color until evenly colored. Repeat with 1¼ cups coconut and 2 to 3 drops green food color. Sprinkle pink coconut over ears and bow tie; outline with candy pieces. Decorate bunny face with jelly beans for eyes, nose and mouth, and string licorice for whiskers. Sprinkle green coconut evenly around cake.

HIGH ALTITUDE (ABOVE 3500 FEET):
See package for directions.

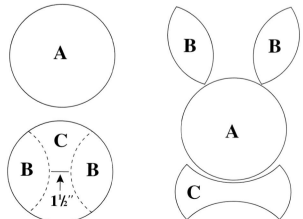

CINNAMON PULL APART

Yield: 8 servings
Prep Time: 10 minutes (Ready in 40 minutes)

1   (12.4-oz.) can Pillsbury Cinnamon Rolls with Icing

1. Heat oven to 375°F. Grease 9x5 or 8x4-inch loaf pan. Separate dough into 8 rolls. Cut each roll into quarters; place in greased pan.

2. Bake at 375°F for 20 to 28 minutes or until top is golden brown. Immediately remove from pan; place on serving plate. Drizzle or spread icing over hot loaf. Serve warm.

STRAWBERRIES AND CREAM PIE

Yield: 12 servings   Prep Time: 30 minutes
(Ready in 1 hour, 50 minutes)

CRUST

1   Pillsbury Refrigerated Pie Crust (from 15-oz. pkg.)

FILLING

1   (8-oz.) pkg. cream cheese, softened
⅓   cup sugar
¼   to ½ teaspoon almond extract
1   cup whipping cream, whipped
2   pints (4 cups) strawberries

GARNISH

½   cup semi-sweet chocolate chips
1   tablespoon shortening

1. Heat oven to 450°F. Prepare pie crust as directed on package for one-crust baked shell using 9-inch pie pan or 10-inch tart pan with removable bottom. Bake at 450°F for 9 to 11 minutes or until light golden brown. Cool 30 minutes or until completely cooled.

2. In large bowl, beat cream cheese until fluffy. Gradually add sugar and almond extract, blending well. Fold in whipped cream. Spoon into cooled baked shell. Arrange strawberries, pointed side up, over filling. Refrigerate while preparing garnish.

3. In small saucepan, melt chocolate chips and shortening over low heat, stirring constantly until smooth. Drizzle over strawberries and filling. Refrigerate 1 hour or until set. Store in refrigerator.

SOUR CREAM POUND CAKE

Yield: 16 servings   Prep Time: 15 minutes
(Ready in 2 hours, 35 minutes)

2¾   cups sugar
1½   cups butter, softened
1   teaspoon vanilla
6   eggs
3   cups Pillsbury BEST® or Martha White® All Purpose Flour
1   teaspoon grated orange or lemon peel
½   teaspoon baking powder
½   teaspoon salt
1   cup sour cream

1. Heat oven to 350°F. Generously butter and flour a 12-cup Bundt® pan. In large bowl, beat sugar and butter until light and fluffy. Add vanilla and eggs one at a time, beating well after each addition.

2. Lightly spoon flour into measuring cup; level off. In medium bowl, combine flour, orange peel, baking powder and salt. Add dry ingredients alternately with sour cream, beating well after each addition. Pour batter into buttered and floured pan.

3. Bake at 350°F for 55 to 65 minutes or until toothpick inserted in center comes out clean. Cool 15 minutes; invert onto serving plate. Cool 1 hour or until completely cooled.

HIGH ALTITUDE (ABOVE 3500 FEET):
Decrease sugar to 2½ cups. Bake at 375°F for 55 to 65 minutes.

Bundt® is a registered trademark of Northland Aluminum Products, Inc., Minneapolis, MN.

Whipping or heavy cream doubles in size when it is whipped. Start with thoroughly chilled whipping cream, bowl and beaters. Beat whipping cream until it thickens. Blend in sugar and flavorings, continuing to beat until soft peaks form. Whipped cream sweetened with powdered sugar is more stable because of the starch in the powdered sugar.

SPRING SEAFOOD LUNCHEON

A delicious selection of simple yet elegant recipes for a perfect springtime luncheon.

STONE MANOR

Middletown, Maryland

*S*tone Manor, located in Middletown, Maryland, dates back to 1760, when the Creager family, who emigrated from Germany in the 1740's, built the stone farmhouse on 114 acres of unspoiled farmland. For over two centuries the private house and land remained a residence, with each owner adding to and remodeling various sections of the structure. Stone Manor began its existence as a restaurant and inn in December 1991.

Today, the Stone Manor is a testimony to the beauty of combining the old with the new. The tasteful decor and comfortable furnishings, some antiques, along with thoroughly modern conveniences, speak to a timeless elegance.

The inn's six lovely suites, some with fireplaces, are beautifully appointed to provide the utmost in comfort and country elegance for its guests.

The elegant dining rooms at Stone Manor offer the finest in American cuisine. The inn's chef prepares dishes with locally grown produce accentuated by fresh herbs picked from the inn's herb garden.

The Stone Manor offers the peace and solitude that one can only find in a rural setting.

STONE MANOR BASIL BUTTER

Yield: 1 cup   Prep Time: 15 minutes

1 teaspoon olive oil	½ teaspoon salt
2 teaspoons minced garlic	½ teaspoon white pepper
½ cup finely chopped fresh basil	¼ teaspoon dry mustard
2 tablespoons red wine	2 tablespoons lemon juice
1 cup (2 sticks) butter, softened	

1. In small skillet, heat oil until hot. Add garlic; cook 1 minute. Add basil and wine; cook until dry. Refrigerate about 10 minutes or until thoroughly chilled.

2. In small bowl, whip butter until light and fluffy. Add basil mixture, salt, pepper and dry mustard; beat well. Stir in lemon juice until well mixed.

3. Serve over cooked vegetables such as green beans, carrots or asparagus, or use in Cod, Shrimp and Snow Peas with Basil Butter recipe, which appears on page 28.

COD, SHRIMP AND SNOW PEAS WITH BASIL BUTTER

Yield: 8 servings
Prep Time: 25 minutes

¾ *pound snow peas, trimmed*

2 *pounds cod fillets*

1 *cup chicken broth*

½ *cup Basil Butter (see recipe for Stone Manor Basil Butter)*

2 *tablespoons water*

¾ *pound fresh large shrimp, peeled, deveined*

3 *medium tomatoes, peeled, seeded and chopped (1 cup)*

½ *teaspoon salt*

¼ *teaspoon pepper*

1. Bring large saucepan of salted water to a boil. Add snow peas; cook 20 to 30 seconds or just until crisp-tender. Drain; immediately plunge into ice water. Drain thoroughly.

2. Divide cod into 8 pieces. In 12-inch nonstick skillet, bring chicken broth and ¼ cup of the Basil Butter to a boil over high heat. Add cod; sprinkle with ¼ teaspoon salt and ⅛ teaspoon pepper. Reduce heat to medium; cover and cook 6 to 7 minutes.

3. While cod is cooking, in large nonstick skillet, heat remaining ¼ cup basil butter and water over high heat until hot. Add shrimp and tomatoes; sprinkle with remaining ¼ teaspoon salt and ⅛ teaspoon pepper. Cook 2½ to 3 minutes. Add snow peas; cook about 2 minutes or until thoroughly heated.

4. To serve, spoon shrimp and tomato mixture evenly onto 8 individual soup/pasta plates; place cod on top.

Store ripe tomatoes
at room temperature
and use within a few days.

To peel a tomato easily,
place in boiling water
for 30 seconds. Remove tomato
and drop in cool water.
Remove skin.

Fresh herbs are best harvested
early in the day, snipping
the amount you need
with a garden or
kitchen shears. Store them,
unwashed and dry, in a
tightly-covered plastic wrap
or container in the
refrigerator vegetable crisper.
Wash fresh herbs before
using them, rinsing lightly and
patting dry on paper towels.

DARK CHOCOLATE PATÉ WITH CRÈME ANGLAISE AND FRESH RASPBERRIES

Yield: 16 servings (2½ cups crème anglaise)
Prep Time: 25 minutes (Ready in 8 hours, 25 minutes)

PATÉ

16 *ounces bittersweet chocolate, chopped*

1 *cup heavy cream*

¼ *cup (½ stick) butter*

4 *egg yolks*

2 *tablespoons dark rum*

CRÈME ANGLAISE

2 *cups milk*

4 *egg yolks*

¾ *cup sugar*

½ *teaspoon vanilla*

TOPPING

Fresh raspberries

Fresh mint leaves, if desired

1. Line 8x4-inch loaf pan or mold with plastic wrap. In small saucepan, combine chocolate, cream and butter; cook over low heat until melted. With wire whisk, beat in 4 egg yolks and rum until smooth. Pour into pan lined with plastic wrap. Refrigerate at least 8 hours or overnight to set.

2. To prepare crème anglaise, in small saucepan, heat milk just until it comes to a simmer. Meanwhile, in medium bowl, beat 4 egg yolks, sugar and vanilla until well blended.

3. Add small amount of hot milk to yolk-sugar mixture, beating constantly. Add remaining milk; cook over low heat, stirring constantly, until mixture is slightly thickened and coats back of spoon. Immediately place saucepan in ice bath to cool. (Sauce will continue to thicken as it cools.)

4. To serve, unmold paté; bring to room temperature before slicing. Cut paté into slices. Spoon crème anglaise onto individual dessert plates. Place slices of paté on plates. Top each with raspberries; garnish with mint leaves.

29

CHILDREN'S BIRTHDAY PARTY

*T*hese charming big-eared, long-whiskered Mini Mouse Party Cupcakes can set the mood for invitations, setting and games for a birthday party to delight "pint-sized" party-goers. You make them ahead and freeze them so they are ready and waiting for just the right serving time. Crescent Dogs and Corn-on-the-Cob Pops are also especially easy for smaller hands to manage and enjoy. Add a beverage of your birthday child's choice along with Kids' Favorite Fruit Salad and your menu is complete.

KIDS' FAVORITE FRUIT SALAD

Yield: 8 (⅔-cup) servings   Prep Time: 15 minutes

1	(17-oz.) can fruit cocktail, drained
1½	cups miniature marshmallows
¼	cup drained maraschino cherries, halved
2	medium bananas, sliced
1	medium apple, coarsely chopped
1½	cups sweetened whipped cream
	Lettuce leaves

1. In large bowl, combine all ingredients except whipped topping and lettuce; mix lightly. Gently fold in whipped topping. Serve immediately, or cover and refrigerate until serving time.

2. To serve, spoon salad onto lettuce-lined plates. If desired, garnish with additional maraschino cherries.

When all the party foods are ready and waiting, all your attention can be given to the young guests. Two hours before the party, Crescent Dogs can be assembled, covered with plastic wrap and refrigerated until time to bake. Meanwhile, the fruit salad can be made and refrigerated and the honey butter can be mixed up for the Corn-on-the-Cob Pops.

CRESCENT DOGS

Yield: 8 sandwiches   Prep Time: 10 minutes
(Ready in 25 minutes)

8	hot dogs
4	slices American cheese, cut into 6 strips each
1	(8-oz.) can Pillsbury Refrigerated Crescent Dinner Rolls

1. Slit hot dogs to within ½ inch of ends; insert 3 strips of cheese into each slit.

2. Separate dough into triangles. Wrap dough triangle around each hot dog. Place on ungreased cookie sheet, cheese side up.

3. Bake at 375°F for 12 to 15 minutes or until golden brown.

CORN-ON-THE-COB POPS

Yield: 6 servings   Prep Time: 10 minutes

6	Green Giant® Nibblers® Frozen Corn-on-the-Cob
3	tablespoons butter, softened
1	teaspoon honey
6	round wooden sticks with one pointed end

1. Cook corn as directed on package.

2. Meanwhile, in small bowl, combine butter and honey; mix well. Insert sticks into corn. Serve with butter mixture.

MINI MOUSE PARTY CUPCAKES

Yield: 8 servings   Prep Time: 30 minutes (Ready in 2 hours)

CUPCAKES

 1 pkg. Pillsbury Moist Supreme® Devil's Food Cake Mix

1¼ cups water

 ½ cup oil

 3 eggs

TOPPING

 8 scoops Häagen-Dazs® Vanilla Ice Cream

16 chocolate sandwich cookies or mints

    Small candies

    String licorice

1. Heat oven to 350°F. Line 24 muffin cups with paper baking cups. Prepare cake mix as directed on package. Fill paper-lined muffin cups ⅔ full.

2. Bake at 350°F for 20 to 30 minutes or until cupcakes spring back when touched lightly in center. Remove from pans; cool 1 hour or until completely cooled.

3. Remove paper baking cups from 8 cupcakes; set aside. (Wrap and freeze remaining cupcakes for later use.)

4. Decorate each ice cream scoop to resemble a mouse, using 2 cookies for ears and small candies and licorice for facial features and whiskers. Place cupcakes in 8 serving bowls. Top each cupcake with decorated ice cream. Freeze until serving time.

HIGH ALTITUDE (ABOVE 3500 FEET):
Add 4 tablespoons flour to dry cake mix. Increase water to 1⅓ cups. Bake at 375°F for 10 to 20 minutes.

MOTHER'S DAY

Make this day extra special by preparing any of these fabulous recipes.

MAIN STREET INN

Hilton Head, South Carolina

The luxurious Main Street Inn is located on the island of Hilton Head, South Carolina.

The Inn was opened in 1996 and patterned after the mansions of antebellum Charleston. Decorated with wrought iron railings and surrounded by spectacular flowering gardens, the Main Street Inn has created the atmosphere of an elegant private mansion with an emphasis on true luxury.

Each of the 34 unique guest rooms are adorned with one-of-a-kind furnishings and accented with fine art works. Beds are lavished with imported linens and feather-filled duvets.

Whether you prefer a cozy double guest room or a lavish courtyard King, with private walled garden and spacious sitting room, your every whim is graciously indulged.

Guests of the inn are invited to enjoy the executive chef's home-made specialties served daily in the tea room, the dining library, and the breakfast area.

The Main Street Inn is the perfect location for a romantic getaway, offering all the luxuries of true Southern hospitality.

RAISIN COOKIES

Yield: About 8 dozen tea cookies   Prep Time: 1 hour, 10 minutes

1   cup (2 sticks) unsalted butter, softened
4   cups powdered sugar
½   cup all-purpose flour

2   tablespoons cornstarch
⅛   teaspoon salt
2   cups raisins

1. Heat oven to 350°F. Line cookie sheets with parchment paper or butter cookie sheets.

2. In large bowl, beat butter until light and fluffy. Add powdered sugar, flour, cornstarch and salt; mix until dough forms. Stir in raisins. Roll dough into balls, using 1 teaspoon dough for each; place on lined cookie sheets.

3. Bake at 350°F for 5 to 7 minutes or until light golden brown around edges. (Surface of cookies will be very light.) Immediately remove from cookie sheets to cool.

SCONES

Yield: 8 servings   Prep Time: 15 minutes (Ready in 40 minutes)

2 cups all-purpose flour	3 tablespoons unsalted butter, cut into pieces
2 tablespoons sugar	1 cup heavy cream
2 tablespoons baking powder	

1. Heat oven to 375°F. In large bowl, combine flour, sugar and baking powder; mix well. Using pastry blender, cut in butter until crumbly. Add cream; mix until dough forms.

2. On floured surface, knead dough 5 or 6 times. Press into 8-inch round; place on ungreased cookie sheet. Cut into 8 wedges; do not separate.

3. Bake at 375°F for 18 to 23 minutes or until light golden brown. Cut into wedges; serve warm.

LEMON CURD

Yield: 1 cup   Prep Time: 20 minutes

2 lemons	2 eggs, beaten
½ cup (1 stick) unsalted butter	Scones (see recipe for Scones)
1 cup sugar	

1. Grate, peel and squeeze lemons; reserve peel and juice.

2. In small saucepan, melt butter. Add sugar; cook until dissolved. With wire whisk, beat in eggs, lemon juice and peel; cook until mixture is thick and coats back of spoon. Cover; refrigerate. Serve with scones.

PIZZA PARTY

✿ ✿

*W*hether savory or sweet, pizza is a favorite food, especially for parties.
As guests enjoy plenty of chilled beverages while chatting,
playing games or watching videos, these recipes can be served in courses to
satisfy hungry appetites. Start with Layered Pizza Dip,
then serve up the Pepper Biscuit Pull-Apart. Have your guests
help assemble Stuffed Crust Pepperoni Pizza as part of the activity of the
party. Fanciful Fruit Pizza can be made ahead and stored in the
refrigerator until time for dessert.

PEPPER BISCUIT PULL-APART

Yield: 10 servings
Prep Time: 20 minutes
(Ready in 35 minutes)

¼ teaspoon garlic powder	4½ teaspoons olive oil
¼ teaspoon salt, if desired	¼ cup chopped green bell pepper
¼ teaspoon dried basil leaves, crushed	¼ cup chopped red bell pepper
¼ teaspoon dried oregano leaves, crushed	1 oz. (¼ cup) shredded Mozzarella cheese
1 (12-oz.) can Hungry Jack® Refrigerated Flaky Biscuits	2 tablespoons grated Romano or Parmesan cheese

1. Heat oven to 400°F. In small bowl, combine garlic powder, salt, basil and oregano; mix well.

2. Separate dough into 10 biscuits. Place 1 biscuit in center of ungreased cookie sheet. Arrange remaining biscuits in circle, edges slightly overlapping, around center biscuit. Gently press out into a 10-inch round.

3. Brush biscuits with oil. Top with bell peppers and cheeses. Sprinkle garlic powder mixture over top.

4. Bake at 400°F for 12 to 15 minutes or until golden brown. To serve, pull apart warm biscuits.

FANCIFUL FRUIT PIZZA

Yield: 12 servings   Prep Time: 20 minutes
(Ready in 1 hour, 45 minutes)

1 (18-oz.) pkg. Pillsbury Refrigerated Sugar Cookies	1 cup whole strawberries, cut in half*
1 (8-oz.) pkg. cream cheese, softened	1 cup fresh or frozen blueberries*
⅓ cup sugar	¼ cup orange marmalade
½ teaspoon vanilla	1 tablespoon water
1 cup fresh or canned peach slices, drained*	

1. Heat oven to 350°F. Slice cookie dough as directed on package. Arrange slices in bottom of ungreased 15x10x1-inch baking pan or 14-inch pizza pan. Using floured fingers, press dough evenly in pan.

2. Bake at 350°F for 12 to 15 minutes or until golden brown. Cool 15 minutes or until completely cooled.

3. In small bowl, beat cream cheese, sugar and vanilla until fluffy. Spread mixture over cooled cookie crust. Arrange fruit over cream cheese.

4. In another small bowl, combine orange marmalade and water; blend well. Spoon marmalade mixture over fruit. Refrigerate at least 1 hour before serving. Cut into squares or wedges. Store in refrigerator.

TIP:
*Other fruit such as fresh or canned pineapple slices, maraschino cherries, mandarin orange segments or sliced peeled kiwi fruit can be used.

STUFFED CRUST PEPPERONI PIZZA

Yield: 6 servings   Prep Time: 15 minutes
(Ready in 30 minutes)

1   (10-oz.) can Pillsbury Refrigerated All Ready Pizza Crust
7   pieces string cheese
½   cup pizza sauce

20   slices pepperoni
4   oz. (1 cup) shredded Mozzarella cheese

1. Heat oven to 425°F. Butter 13x9-inch pan. Unroll dough and press in bottom and 1-inch up sides of buttered pan.

2. Place pieces of string cheese along inside edges of dough. Fold 1 inch of dough over and around cheese; press dough edges to seal. Top crust with pizza sauce, pepperoni and cheese.

3. Bake at 425°F for 15 to 18 minutes or until crust is golden brown and cheese is melted.

LAYERED PIZZA DIP

Yield: 2 cups   Prep Time: 10 minutes
(Ready in 25 minutes)

1   (8-oz.) container soft cream cheese with chives and onions
½   cup chunky pizza sauce
½   cup chopped green bell pepper

2   oz. (½ cup) shredded Mozzarella cheese
2   oz. (½ cup) shredded Cheddar cheese

1. Heat oven to 350°F. In ungreased 9-inch pie pan or 1 to 1½-quart baking dish, layer all ingredients in order listed.

2. Bake at 350°F for 10 to 15 minutes or until dip is hot and cheese is melted.

3. Serve warm with bagel crisps, bagel chips or crackers.

SUNDAY BRUNCH

A collection of easy and delicious recipes to include in your summertime entertaining.

CASA MADRONA

Sausalito, California

*T*he charming Casa Madrona Hotel is located in Sausalito, California. Majestically situated high on a hillside, the 1885 Victorian house, decorated with beautiful antiques, is a tribute to a bygone era. The guest rooms, many with a view of the bay, are fashionably appointed and offer the ultimate in comfort.

The newly added surrounding cottages and hillside casitas also provide guests with luxurious accommodations.

dreamlike ambiance of faraway places and ancient cultures. The focal wall in the dining room has a stunning twelve-foot mural of the Goddess Mikayla gazing out to sea. Legend speaks of Mikayla's gift of nourishment to villagers in times of need.

Mikayla's executive chef uses only the area's freshest ingredients. Guests may sample his creations during nightly dinners and scrumptious Sunday Brunches.

The hotel dining room has been transformed into the stunning, magical Mikayla restaurant. Mikayla has a warm,

The Casa Madrona proudly offers its guests all the comfort and service of gracious West Coast hospitality.

POTATO GRATIN

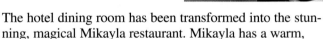

Yield: 6 to 8 servings   Prep Time: 20 minutes (Ready in 1 hour)

2	cups heavy cream	1¼	teaspoons salt
2	tablespoons butter	½	teaspoon pepper
2	garlic cloves, minced	½	cup (2 ounces) shredded Cheddar cheese
5	large Yukon gold or red potatoes, peeled, thinly sliced		

1. Heat oven to 375°F. In large saucepan, combine cream, butter and garlic; heat over medium heat until hot. Add potatoes; cook until tender, about 15 to 20 minutes, stirring occasionally.

2. Stir in salt and pepper. Spoon potatoes and sauce into ungreased 12x8-inch (2-quart) baking dish; spread evenly. Sprinkle with cheese.

3. Bake at 375°F for 15 to 20 minutes or until bubbly.

SAVORY CHEDDAR CHEESE BISCUITS

Yield: 30 biscuits   Prep Time: 25 minutes
(Ready in 45 minutes)

3	cups all-purpose flour	2	cups milk or light cream
3	tablespoons sugar	½	cup (2 ounces) shredded Cheddar cheese
4½	teaspoons baking powder	½	cup thinly sliced green onions
1	teaspoon salt		
½	cup (1 stick) butter, cut into pieces		

1. Heat oven to 375°F. Butter cookie sheets. In large bowl, combine flour, sugar, baking powder and salt; blend well. Using pastry blender or fork, cut in butter until mixture is crumbly. Add milk; stir just until moistened. Gently stir in cheese and green onions.

2. To form each biscuit, drop dough by tablespoonfuls onto buttered cookie sheets.

3. Bake at 375°F for 15 to 20 minutes or until light golden brown. Serve warm.

Butter Makes Breads Better

Butter not only makes a marvelous spread for breads, it also adds rich flavor and contributes to a tender texture when used as an ingredient in homemade breads.

For best results, follow recipes exactly and measure correctly. Use appropriate measuring utensils. To easily measure butter, use the markings often on the wrapper.

When baking, always check food at the end of the minimum baking time to determine doneness–baking time can vary depending upon the oven.

The Key to Great Taste

If you want to get creative in the kitchen, start with butter. No matter what you do, your creations are bound to come out well, because butter makes everything taste better.

SCRAMBLED EGGS PIPÉRADE

Yield: 4 servings   Prep Time: 25 minutes

PIPÉRADE

2   *tablespoons butter*

½   *cup thinly sliced onion*

½   *cup thinly sliced ham, cut into thin strips*

1   *garlic clove, minced*

½   *cup peeled seeded chopped tomatoes*

EGGS

2   *tablespoons butter*

6   *eggs, beaten*

¼   *teaspoon salt*

¼   *teaspoon pepper*

⅛   *teaspoon paprika*

4   *tablespoons milk*

1. In large skillet, over medium heat, melt butter. Add onions and green pepper; saute 1 to 2 minutes or until vegetables are crisp-tender. Add tomatoes; heat until warm. Cover; set aside.

2. In another large skillet, melt 2 tablespoons butter. Meanwhile in medium bowl, combine remaining ingredients; add to butter. Cook until eggs are set but still moist, stirring occasionally from outside edge to center of pan. Spoon eggs onto platter; top with Pipérade and serve warm.

GRADUATION PARTY

*W*ith diploma in hand, graduates are always ready to celebrate!
This festive fare is appropriate for patio, deck or porch. All recipes can be made
and refrigerated well before the party begins which is a definite advantage on party days.
Add chilled beverages or punch and your menu is complete. The Crowd-Sized Sandwich
is a welcome change of pace for gatherings and perfectly complemented with refreshing
Melon Medley. Chocolate Toffee Caramel Bars, a Bake-off® Contest winning recipe, are
buttery rich and irresistibly everyone's favorite sweet treat.

CREAMY SPINACH DIP

Yield: 3½ cups   Prep Time: 20 minutes
(Ready in 2 hours, 20 minutes)

1	(10-oz.) pkg. Green Giant® Harvest Fresh® Frozen Spinach
1	(8-oz.) container sour cream
1	cup mayonnaise
½	teaspoon celery salt
½	teaspoon dried dill weed
¼	teaspoon onion salt
¼	cup chopped green onions
3	tablespoons chopped pimientos or red bell pepper, if desired
1	(8-oz.) can water chestnuts, drained, finely chopped

1. Cook spinach as directed on package. Cool; squeeze to drain.

2. In medium bowl, combine sour cream, mayonnaise, celery salt, dill and onion salt; blend well.

3. Stir in spinach, onions, pimientos and water chestnuts. Cover; refrigerate at least 2 hours to blend flavors. Serve with assorted crackers or cut-up fresh vegetables.

CROWD-SIZED SANDWICH

Yield: 20 servings   Prep Time: 15 minutes
(Ready in 2 hours, 15 minutes)

SANDWICH

2	(1-lb.) loaves French bread (14 inches long)
2	cups chopped lettuce
½	lb. thinly sliced cooked roast beef
6	oz. thinly sliced smoked turkey
6	oz. thinly sliced cooked ham

DRESSING

½	cup mayonnaise
½	cup sour cream
1	tablespoon milk
1	tablespoon Dijon mustard
1	teaspoon dried dill weed
¼	teaspoon garlic powder

1. Slice each loaf in half lengthwise. Place 1 cup of the lettuce on bottom half of each loaf. Arrange rolled or folded meat slices over lettuce, alternating beef, turkey and ham. Wrap top and bottom halves of each loaf in plastic wrap. Refrigerate at least 2 hours or until serving time.

2. In small bowl, combine all dressing ingredients; blend until smooth. Refrigerate to blend flavors.

3. Just before serving, spoon dressing over meat slices; cover with top halves of loaves. Cut each loaf into 10 slices.

CHOCOLATE-TOFFEE CARAMEL BARS

Yield: 24 bars   Prep Time: 30 minutes (Ready in 3 hours)

1 *pkg. Pillsbury Moist Supreme®* *Butter Recipe Yellow Cake Mix*	3 *(1.4-oz.) chocolate-covered toffee* *candy bars, cut into pieces*
⅓ *cup oil*	½ *cup butter*
2 *eggs*	32 *vanilla caramels, unwrapped*
1 *(12-oz.) pkg. (2 cups) semi-sweet* *chocolate chips*	1 *(14-oz.) can sweetened condensed* *milk (not evaporated)*
1 *cup white vanilla chips*	

1. Heat oven to 350°F. Grease 13x9-inch pan. In large bowl, combine cake mix, oil and eggs; blend well. Stir in chocolate chips, vanilla chips and candy bar pieces. (Mixture will be thick.) Press half of mixture in bottom of greased pan. Bake at 350°F for 10 minutes.

2. Meanwhile, in medium saucepan, combine butter, caramels and sweetened condensed milk. Cook over medium-low heat until caramels are melted and mixture is smooth, stirring occasionally. Slowly pour caramel mixture evenly over partially baked crust. Top with remaining cake mix mixture.

3. Bake an additional 25 to 30 minutes or until top is set and edges are deep golden brown. Cool 20 minutes. Run knife around sides of pan to loosen. Cool 40 minutes. Refrigerate 1 hour. Cut into bars. Store in refrigerator.

MELON MEDLEY

Yield: 12 (½-cup) servings   Prep Time: 25 minutes

¼ *cup honey*	2 *tablespoons lime juice*
1 *teaspoon grated orange peel*	1 *tablespoon chopped fresh mint leaves*
1 *teaspoon grated lime peel*	6 *cups assorted melon balls or*
½ *cup orange juice*	*cubes (cantaloupe, honeydew* *and/or watermelon)*

1. In small bowl, combine all ingredients except melon balls; mix well.

2. Place melon balls in serving bowl. Pour honey mixture over melon; toss gently to coat. Serve immediately or refrigerate until serving time.

SUMMER LUNCHEON

Plan the perfect summer luncheon with these delicious recipes.

CASTLE MARNE

Denver, Colorado

Castle Marne Bed & Breakfast is located in Denver, Colorado.

The rustic lava-stone mansion was originally built as a private residence in 1889 and is one of Denver's grandest historic mansions.

The fabulous ambiance of Castle Marne, with its renowned circular stain glass peacock window and graciously decorated rooms, celebrates the old world elegance and charm of the Victorian era, combined with the luxuries and conveniences of today.

Each morning, Castle Marne guests awake to the spicy aroma of brewing coffee — a special Marne-blend. Gourmet breakfasts are prepared with the freshest of seasonal ingredients and served in the original formal dining room, at tables set with white linen, china, crystal, and silver. The inn also prepares lovely candle-lit dinners for its guests in the formal dining room.

A visit to Castle Marne with its fairy tale ambiance guarantees its guests a romantic getaway long to be remembered.

DOROTHEA'S CRAB DELIGHT

Yield: 4 (¾-cup) servings   Prep Time: 15 minutes (Ready in 45 minutes)

1   cup (4 ounces) shredded Cheddar cheese

1   cup mayonnaise

½   cup grated onion, drained

1   (6-ounce) can crabmeat, drained, flaked

¼   teaspoon curry powder

6   drops hot pepper sauce

2   tablespoons dry bread crumbs
     Toast points

1. Heat oven to 350°F. Butter 1-quart casserole.

2. In medium bowl, combine all ingredients except bread crumbs. Spoon mixture into buttered casserole. Sprinkle with bread crumbs.

3. Bake at 350°F for 25 to 30 minutes or until bubbly. Serve with toast points.

TOMATO CURRY SOUP

Yield: 6 to 8 (1¼-cup) servings   Prep Time: 30 minutes

¼ cup (½ stick) butter
½ cup chopped onion
2½ teaspoons curry powder
1 (28-ounce) can crushed tomatoes, undrained

4 cups chicken broth
½ cup sour cream
   Sour cream
   Chopped fresh parsley

1. Melt butter in medium saucepan. Add onion; cook until tender. Add curry powder; cook an additional minute to blend flavors.

2. Stir in tomatoes and broth. Bring to a boil. Reduce heat; simmer 15 to 20 minutes.

3. Add ½ cup sour cream; let melt into soup. With wire whisk, beat soup until smooth. Garnish each serving with small dollop of additional sour cream; sprinkle with parsley.

DAME MARGARET'S LEMON BARS

Yield: 24 to 30 bars   Prep Time: 15 minutes
(Ready in 1 hour, 35 minutes)

CRUST

- 2   cups all-purpose flour
- 1   cup (2 sticks) butter, softened
- ½   cup powdered sugar

FILLING

- 2   cups sugar
- ¼   cup all-purpose flour
- 1   teaspoon baking powder
- ½   cup fresh lemon juice
- 4   eggs

1. Heat oven to 350°F. In medium bowl, combine butter and 2 cups flour; cut in butter until coarse crumbs form. Stir in powdered sugar. Press mixture in bottom of unbuttered 13x9-inch pan. Bake at 350°F for 10 to 12 minutes or until golden brown around edges.

2. Meanwhile, in another medium bowl, combine sugar, ¼ cup flour, baking powder, lemon juice and eggs; beat well. Pour over baked crust.

3. Bake at 350°F for an additional 18 to 23 minutes. Cool 1 hour. Sprinkle with additional powdered sugar. Cut into bars.

THE DUTCHESS' RASPBERRY BARS

nice
12 10-99

Yield: 24 to 30 bars
Prep Time: 20 minutes (Ready in 2 hours)

CRUST

- 1   (1 pound 2.25-ounce) package white or yellow cake mix
- ½   cup (1 stick) butter, softened

LAYER

- ½   cup raspberry preserves

FILLING

- 1   (8-ounce) package cream cheese, softened
- ¼   cup sugar
- 2   tablespoons all-purpose flour
- 1   teaspoon vanilla
- 1   egg
- ¼   cup raspberry preserves

1. Heat oven to 350°F. Butter 13x9-inch pan. In large bowl, combine cake mix and butter; mix with fork until crumbly. Reserve 1 cup for topping. Press remaining mixture in bottom of buttered pan. Carefully spread ½ cup preserves over crust.

2. In medium bowl, combine cream cheese, sugar, flour, vanilla, egg and ¼ cup preserves; mix until well blended. Spread evenly over preserves layer. Sprinkle with reserved topping.

3. Bake at 350°F for 30 to 40 minutes. Cool at least 1 hour or until completely cooled. Cut into bars.

THE QUEEN'S CHICKEN DIJON

Yield: 4 servings
Prep Time: 20 minutes

- 3   tablespoons butter
- 4   (4 to 6-ounce) boneless skinless chicken breast halves, cut into small thin strips
- 2   tablespoons all-purpose flour
- 1   cup chicken broth
- ½   cup light cream
- 1   tablespoon Dijon mustard
- ¼   teaspoon salt
- ⅛   teaspoon pepper
- 4   baked puff pastry shells
    Coarsely chopped fresh parsley

1. Melt butter in large skillet. Add chicken; cook about 3 minutes or until lightly browned. Remove chicken from skillet; cover to keep warm.

2. With wire whisk, stir flour into drippings in skillet over medium-high heat; cook 1 minute. Add broth and cream; cook and stir until bubbly and thickened. Stir in mustard, salt and pepper.

3. Return chicken to skillet; cook until thoroughly heated. Serve over pastry shells. Garnish with parsley.

FATHER'S DAY FAVORITES

*T*his holiday which falls on the third Sunday of June
is very much a family celebration. What better way to celebrate with Dad
than with a casual gathering featuring grilled meat and potatoes?
Dad may even choose to preside over the grilling or enter into a
rugged game of croquet or bocce ball – or both. Younger hands can help prepare
Foil-Wrapped Potatoes and stir together the Cheddar-Onion Butter that
will top the Grilled Steaks. Serve Creamy Cashew Brownies with scoops of
vanilla ice cream you purchase or make yourself
as the grand finale for a grand day.

DILL BABY CARROTS

Yield: 7 (½-cup) servings
Prep Time: 15 minutes

1	lb. fresh baby carrots	1	teaspoon fresh lemon juice
1	tablespoon butter		
1	teaspoon chopped fresh dill or ¼ teaspoon dried dill weed	¼	teaspoon salt
		⅛	teaspoon pepper

1. In medium saucepan, bring ¾ cup water to a boil. Add carrots; cover and cook over medium heat for 10 to 12 minutes or until tender.

2. Drain carrots; return to saucepan. Add all remaining ingredients; stir until butter is melted.

Dill is a member of the parsley
family. The leaves, called
dill weed, are thin and
feathery with a tart, lemony
flavor. Other herbs and spices
that are compatible with
carrots are mint, chives,
cinnamon, ginger and nutmeg.
In general, if substituting
dry herbs for fresh herbs, use
one-third of the amount called
for in the recipe.

CREAMY CASHEW BROWNIES

Yield: 24 servings   Prep Time: 15 minutes
(Ready in 2 hours)

BASE

1	(1 lb. 5.5-oz.) pkg. Pillsbury Traditional Fudge Brownie Mix
⅓	cup water
¼	cup oil
1	egg
1	cup chocolate chips, if desired

TOPPING

2	(8-oz.) pkg. cream cheese, softened
1	cup powdered sugar
1	teaspoon vanilla
1½	cups cashews or peanuts
½	cup hot fudge ice cream topping, heated

1. Heat oven to 350°F. Grease bottom only of 13x9-inch pan. In large bowl, combine brownie mix, water, oil and egg; beat 50 strokes with spoon. Stir in chocolate chips. Spread in greased pan.

2. Bake at 350°F for 24 to 27 minutes. DO NOT OVERBAKE. Cool 45 minutes or until completely cooled.

3. In medium bowl, combine cream cheese, powdered sugar and vanilla; beat until smooth. Spread over cooled base. Sprinkle cashews over cream cheese mixture. Drizzle with fudge topping. Refrigerate 30 minutes or until serving time. Store in refrigerator.

HIGH ALTITUDE (ABOVE 3500 FEET):
Add 2 tablespoons flour to dry brownie mix. Bake as directed above.

GRILLED STEAKS WITH CHEDDAR-ONION BUTTER

Yield: 4 servings   Prep Time: 25 minutes

CHEDDAR-ONION BUTTER

¼ cup (½ stick) butter, softened

¼ cup sliced green onions

½ teaspoon dry mustard

2 oz. (½ cup) finely shredded Cheddar cheese

STEAKS

4 beef sirloin or T-bone steaks (1 inch thick)

¼ teaspoon salt

¼ teaspoon coarse ground black pepper

GRILLING DIRECTIONS:

1. Heat grill. In small bowl, combine all butter ingredients; mix well. Set aside.

2. When ready to grill, place steaks on gas grill over medium heat or on charcoal grill 4 to 6 inches from medium coals. Cook 10 to 15 minutes or until desired doneness, turning once. During last minute of cooking time, sprinkle steaks with salt and pepper; top each with ¼ of Cheddar-onion butter.

BROILING DIRECTIONS:

1. Prepare butter as directed above. Place steaks on broiler pan.

2. Broil 4 to 6 inches from heat for 10 to 15 minutes, turning once. Continue as directed above.

FOIL-WRAPPED POTATOES

Yield: 4 servings   Prep Time: 15 minutes
(Ready in 1 hour, 10 minutes)

4 medium unpeeled potatoes, cubed (4 cups)

½ cup chopped onion

4 teaspoons chopped fresh parsley

½ teaspoon salt

⅛ teaspoon pepper

¼ cup (½ stick) butter

GRILLING DIRECTIONS:

1. Heat grill. Cut four 18x12-inch pieces of heavy-duty foil. Place ¼ of potatoes and onion on each piece of foil. Sprinkle each with ¼ of parsley, salt and pepper; top each with 1 tablespoon butter. Wrap each packet securely using double-fold seals, allowing room for heat expansion.

2. When ready to grill, place foil packets on gas grill over medium heat or on charcoal grill 4 to 6 inches from medium coals. Cook 45 to 55 minutes or until potatoes are tender, rearranging packets several times during cooking.

OVEN DIRECTIONS:

1. Heat oven to 350°F. Prepare packets as directed above. Place packets, seam side up, in 15x10x1-inch baking pan.

2. Bake at 350°F for 45 to 55 minutes or until potatoes are tender.

SOUTHWEST DINNER

Prepare a fabulous summer dinner with true Southwestern flair!

❧ ❧

WHITE MOUNTAIN LODGE

Greer, Arizona

*T*he White Mountain Lodge is located in Greer, Arizona. This 1892 farmhouse was the residence of one of the first pioneer families in the Greer area. This historic home became the White Mountain Lodge in 1990. The present owners purchased and restored The Lodge in 1993.

The common rooms reflect the home's Southwestern country heritage with period antiques, Southwestern art and mission style furniture. Each bedroom, including its private bath, is individually decorated in Southwestern or country style.

All breakfasts are made from scratch and include homemade baked goods. The menus go from traditional to the extraordinary. The cookie jar is always filled with homemade treats, and coffee, teas, and hot drinks are close at hand all day.

The White Mountain Lodge, surrounded by pine and aspen-covered hills overlooking a gorgeous meadow and the Little Colorado River, affords guests spectacular scenery and unhurried hospitality.

SPICY CHEESE SOUP

Yield: 8 (1-cup) servings   Prep Time: 30 minutes (Ready in 1 hour)

3 poblano chiles, roasted, peeled and chopped,* or ½ (8-ounce) can roasted green chile strips	1 cup chopped celery
	2 medium onions, chopped (1 cup)
3 to 4 pounds red potatoes, peeled, quartered	½ teaspoon salt
	¼ teaspoon garlic powder
2 cups (8 ounces) finely shredded Monterey Jack cheese	⅛ teaspoon pepper
	2 to 4 tablespoons bacon drippings
1 cup thinly sliced leeks, if desired	1 to 2 cups half-and-half or milk

1. Place potatoes in large saucepan; add enough water to cover. Bring to a boil. Cover; cook 20 minutes or until tender.

2. Drain potatoes, reserving cooking liquid. Return potatoes and 3 cups cooking liquid to saucepan; mash potatoes. Add roasted chiles, cheese, leeks, celery, onions, salt, garlic powder, pepper and bacon drippings; mix well. Simmer about 30 minutes or until flavors have blended, and celery and onions are tender.

3. Add half-and-half or milk; cook over low heat until thoroughly heated, stirring frequently to prevent scorching.

TIP:
* To roast chiles, line broiler pan rack with foil; cut holes in foil. Cut chiles in half lengthwise; remove seeds. Place chiles cut side down on foil-lined pan. Broil 4 to 6 inches from heat for 8 to 10 minutes or until skins are charred. Place chiles in brown paper bag for 10 minutes. Peel and discard skin from chile halves; coarsely chop chiles.

CHALUPA

Yield: 20 servings   Prep Time: 20 minutes
(Ready in 8 hours, 20 minutes)

1   (4-pound) pork roast
1   (16-ounce) package dried pinto beans, sorted, rinsed
2   tablespoons chili powder
2   teaspoons salt
3   teaspoons cumin
1   teaspoon ground oregano
2   garlic cloves, chopped

1   (4.5-ounce) can diced green chiles
Flour tortillas
Shredded cheese
Chopped onions
Shredded lettuce
Diced tomatoes
Sour cream
Salsa
Avocado slices

1. In 8-quart stockpot, combine pork roast, beans, chili powder, salt, cumin, oregano, garlic and chiles; cover with water. Cover; cook over low heat for about 6 hours or until pork is very tender and coming off bone, adding water as needed.

2. Remove pork roast from stockpot; shred pork with fork. Return shredded pork to stockpot. Cook uncovered over medium heat for 1 to 2 hours or until thick.

3. Serve pork-bean mixture on tortillas topped with cheese, onions, lettuce, tomatoes, sour cream, salsa and avocado.

TIP:
Pork-bean mixture can be frozen for later use.

FRIJOLES DE RANCHO

Yield: 12 (½-cup) servings
Prep Time: 30 minutes (Ready in 14 hours)

1   (16-ounce) package dried pinto beans, sorted, rinsed
6   cups water
1   medium onion, chopped (1/2 cup)
1   small pork rind or ham bone (about ¼ pound)
2   teaspoons pepper

½   teaspoon salt
2   or 3 garlic cloves, minced
2   teaspoons minced garlic
½   to 1 teaspoon pepper
2   cups (8 ounces) shredded Cheddar cheese
½   cup milk

1. Place beans in Dutch oven or large stockpot; cover with water. Soak at least 12 hours or overnight. Drain.

2. In same Dutch oven or stockpot, combine soaked beans, 6 cups water, onion, pork rind, 2 teaspoons pepper, salt and 2 or 3 minced garlic cloves; stir to mix. Bring to a boil. Reduce heat; cover and simmer 1½ hours or until tender.

3. Remove and discard pork rind and excess liquid. Mash bean mixture with potato masher. Stir in 2 teaspoons minced garlic and ½ to 1 teaspoon pepper. Add cheese and milk; mix well. Simmer over low heat until thoroughly heated and flavors have blended, stirring frequently to prevent scorching. If desired, serve topped with additional cheese.

FLAN

Yield: 6 servings   Prep Time: 25 minutes (Ready in 2 hours, 25 minutes)

1¼   cups sugar
½   teaspoon cinnamon
¼   teaspoon allspice
⅛   teaspoon salt

2   tablespoons cognac
1   teaspoon vanilla
2   eggs
2   cups milk

1. Heat oven to 350°F. Place thin layer of paper towels in bottom of 13x9-inch pan.

2. In heavy skillet, heat ¾ cup of the sugar over medium-high heat for 3 to 4 minutes, stirring constantly, until sugar is melted and golden brown. Divide evenly into six 6-ounce custard cups; let harden in cups.

3. In medium bowl, combine remaining ½ cup sugar, cinnamon, allspice, salt, cognac, vanilla and eggs. Add milk; blend well. Pour custard mixture over caramelized sugar in cups.

4. Place custard cups in paper towel-lined pan so they do not touch. Pour very hot water into pan to within ½ inch of tops of cups.

5. Bake at 350°F for 50 to 60 minutes or until knife inserted in center of cup comes out clean. Cool; refrigerate at least 1 hour or until serving time. To serve, unmold onto dessert plates.

ENCHILADA CASSEROLE

Yield: 6 to 8 servings   Prep Time: 20 minutes (Ready in 55 minutes)

1   (1.5-ounce) package enchilada
    sauce mix

1   (8-ounce) can tomato sauce

1½ cups water

1   (6-ounce) package (12) corn tortillas

1   cup (4 ounces) shredded
    Cheddar cheese

1   cup (4 ounces) shredded
    Monterey Jack cheese

1   pound extra-lean ground beef,
    cooked, drained

1   medium onion, chopped (½ cup)

1   (4-ounce) can diced green
    chiles, drained

1   (11-ounce) can vacuum-packed
    corn, drained

1. Heat oven to 350°F. Prepare enchilada sauce mix as directed on package using tomato sauce and water. Set aside.

2. Tear tortillas into ½-inch strips; place in bottom of ungreased 13x9-inch (3-quart) baking dish. Reserve ½ cup of each cheese for topping. Add enchilada sauce and all remaining ingredients to baking dish; mix well. Sprinkle reserved 1 cup cheese over top of casserole.

3. Bake at 350°F for 30 to 35 minutes. If desired, serve topped with shredded lettuce, diced tomatoes, extra cheese, sour cream and salsa.

FAMILY REUNION

*A*ppetites come in all sizes and all ages when it's family reunion time. An array of easy-to-eat foods and ones that adapt well to patio or park is the order of the day. Everyone can share in the food preparation with recipes like Crispy Herb Chicken and Calico Bean Pot that can easily adjust to the appropriate number in your gathering and are so easy to tote. Be sure to pack foods in well-insulated containers to keep foods hot or cold until ready to serve.

COOKIES 'N CREAM CAKE

Yield: 12 servings   Prep Time: 15 minutes
(Ready in 2 hours, 15 minutes)

1	pkg. Pillsbury Moist Supreme® White Cake Mix
1¼	cups water
¼	cup oil
3	egg whites

1	cup coarsely crushed creme-filled chocolate sandwich cookies
1	can Pillsbury Creamy Supreme® Vanilla Frosting

1. Heat oven to 350°F. Butter and flour 13x9-inch pan. Prepare cake mix as directed on package. Gently stir in cookies. Pour into buttered and floured pan.

2. Bake at 350°F for 30 to 40 minutes or until toothpick inserted in center comes out clean. Cool 1 hour or until completely cooled.

3. Spread frosting over cooled cake. Garnish as desired.

CALYPSO COLESLAW

Yield: 24 (½-cup) servings
Prep Time: 15 minutes
(Ready in 1 hour, 15 minutes)

SLAW

8	cups shredded cabbage
1	cup sliced green onions
4	oz. American cheese, cubed (1 cup)
½	cup sliced ripe olives
2	(11-oz.) cans Green Giant® Mexicorn® Whole Kernel Corn, Red and Green Peppers, drained

DRESSING

2	cups salad dressing or mayonnaise
¼	cup sugar
1	teaspoon celery seed
¼	cup vinegar
2	tablespoons prepared mustard

1. In large bowl, combine all slaw ingredients; toss to combine.

2. In small bowl, combine all dressing ingredients; blend well. Add to slaw, tossing to coat evenly. Cover; refrigerate 1 hour to blend flavors.

CALICO BEAN POT

Yield: 18 (½-cup) servings
Prep Time: 15 minutes
(Ready in 1 hour, 25 minutes)

3   medium onions, chopped

1   tablespoon butter

1   teaspoon garlic powder

1   teaspoon dry mustard

½   cup firmly packed brown sugar

¼   cup cider vinegar

2   (28-oz.) cans B&M® Brick Oven Baked Beans

1   (15.5 or 15-oz.) can Green Giant®, Joan of Arc® or Progresso® Kidney Beans, drained

1   (15.5-oz.) can Green Giant® or Joan of Arc® Butter Beans, drained

1. Heat oven to 350°F. In Dutch oven, cook onions in butter over medium heat until tender.

2. Add all remaining ingredients; mix well. Bake uncovered at 350°F for 60 to 70 minutes or until hot and bubbly.

CRISPY BAKED CHICKEN

Yield: 4 servings Prep Time:10 minutes
(Ready in 1 hour, 10 minutes)

⅔   cup Hungry Jack® Mashed Potato Flakes

⅓   cup grated Parmesan cheese

2   teaspoons parsley flakes

1½   teaspoons Ac´cent® Flavor Enhancer

¾   to 1 teaspoon garlic salt

1   (3 to 3½-lb.) cut-up frying chicken, skinned if desired

⅓   cup (⅔ stick) butter, melted

1. Heat oven to 375°F. Butter or line with foil 15x10x1-inch baking pan or 13x9-inch pan.

2. In medium bowl, combine potato flakes, Parmesan cheese, parsley flakes, Ac´cent® Flavor Enhancer and garlic salt; stir until well mixed. Dip chicken pieces in butter; roll in potato flake mixture to coat. Place in greased pan.

3. Bake at 375°F for 45 to 60 minutes or until chicken is fork-tender and juices run clear.

SUMMER SIDE DISHES

Add a dash of spice to your summer recipe collection.

INN OF THE ANASAZI
Santa Fe, New Mexico

The elegant Inn of the Anasazi is located in Santa Fe, New Mexico. The Inn is an intimate, world-class luxury hotel that celebrates the enduring and creative spirit of the early Native Americans known as the Anasazi.

The Inn's fifty-nine guest rooms are designed in an artful blend of southwestern culture and luxurious comfort. Hand crafted furnishings, four poster beds, and gas lit kiva fireplaces are framed under vegas and latillas - the wooden beams and poles that decoratively support the ceilings of Santa Fe's traditional architecture.

The guest services of the Inn have set new standards in Santa Fe hospitality and possibly the entire Southwest.

The restaurant serves an exciting menu that honors the culinary legacies of the southwest. Dishes are made with natural healthy ingredients including locally grown organic produce.

The living room off the main lobby, warmed by a wood-burning kiva fireplace, is an appropriate setting for intimate social gatherings or just to enjoy a quiet reflective moment.

A stay at the Inn of the Anasazi creates in its guests a renewed sense of connection to the earth and furthers the feeling with a world-class haven in perfect harmony with the history and environment of Santa Fe.

CINNAMON PEAR BUTTER

Yield: ½ cup   Prep Time: 20 minutes

½ cup (1 stick) butter, softened	1 red Anjou pear, very finely chopped
⅛ teaspoon cinnamon	¼ cup firmly packed brown sugar
½ vanilla bean, scraped, or ½ teaspoon vanilla	½ teaspoon grated lemon peel

1. In blender container or food processor bowl with metal blade, combine all ingredients; blend until smooth.
2. Serve on scones or muffins.

51

ORANGE PECAN BRIOCHE

Yield: 12 brioche   Prep Time: 40 minutes (Ready in 3 hours, 20 minutes)

3¾	to 4 cups bread flour	1	pkg. active dry yeast
¾	cup chopped pecans	1	cup milk
2	tablespoons sugar	½	cup (1 stick) butter
2	teaspoons grated orange peel	2	eggs
1¼	teaspoons salt		

1. In large bowl, combine 2 cups of the flour, pecans, sugar, orange peel, salt and yeast; blend well.

2. In small saucepan, heat milk and butter until very warm (120 to 130°F). Add warm liquid and eggs to flour mixture; blend at low speed until moistened. Beat 3 minutes at medium speed, scraping down sides of bowl occasionally. By hand, stir in 1 to 1½ cups flour until dough pulls cleanly away from sides of bowl.

3. On floured surface, knead dough 10 minutes or until dough is smooth and elastic. Place dough in buttered bowl; cover loosely with buttered plastic wrap and cloth towel. Let rise in warm place (80 to 85°F) until doubled in size, 1 to 1½ hours.

4. Butter 12 muffin cups. Punch down dough to remove all air bubbles. Divide dough into 12 equal pieces; shape into balls. Place 1 ball in each buttered muffin cup. Cover; let rise in warm place until doubled in size, 35 to 45 minutes.

5. Heat oven to 375°F. Uncover dough. Bake 22 to 25 minutes or until rolls are golden brown and sound hollow when lightly tapped. Immediately remove from pan. Serve warm.

WHITE CHEDDAR CHIPOTLE MASHED POTATOES

Yield: 7 (½-cup) servings
Prep Time: 30 minutes

4 (6 to 8-ounce) baking potatoes, peeled, diced

1½ teaspoons minced roasted garlic*

1 cup (4 ounces) shredded white Cheddar cheese

4 ounces (¼ cup) cream cheese, softened

5 dried chipotle chiles, rehydrated, chopped**

2 tablespoons heavy cream

2 tablespoons butter

¾ teaspoon salt

1. Place potatoes in large saucepan; add enough water to cover. Bring to a boil. Reduce heat; cook about 20 minutes or until tender. Drain.

2. Beat potatoes until smooth. Add cream cheese; beat well. Fold in all remaining ingredients; cook until thoroughly heated.

TIPS:
*To roast fresh garlic cloves, place 3 garlic cloves on cookie sheet; bake at 350°F for 30 to 40 minutes or until tender. Cool; finely chop to yield 1½ teaspoons.

**To rehydrate chipotle chiles, bring 2 cups water to a boil. Add chiles; let soak for 15 to 20 minutes or until softened. Drain; finely chop.

WHIPPED GREEN CHILE SWEET POTATOES

Yield: 12 (½-cup) servings
Prep Time: 30 minutes

4 (6 to 8-ounce) large sweet potatoes

½ cup firmly packed brown sugar

¼ cup (½ stick) unsalted butter, softened

¼ cup milk

1 teaspoon chopped fresh thyme

½ teaspoon salt

¼ teaspoon pepper

4 Anaheim chiles, roasted, peeled and chopped,* or ⅔ cup canned peeled, roasted green chile strips, chopped

1. Peel and dice sweet potatoes; place in large saucepan. Add enough water to cover. Bring to a boil. Reduce heat; cover and simmer about 10 to 15 minutes or until tender but not overcooked.

2. Place cooked potatoes in large bowl. With electric mixer, beat potatoes until smooth. Add all remaining ingredients except chiles; fold in until butter is melted. Fold in chiles.

TIP:
*To roast chiles, line broiler pan rack with foil; cut holes in foil. Cut Anaheim chiles in half lengthwise; remove seeds. Place chiles cut side down on foil-lined pan. Broil 4 to 6 inches from heat for 8 to 10 minutes or until skins are charred. Place chiles in brown paper bag for 10 minutes. Peel and discard skin from chile halves; coarsely chop chiles.

Store garlic in a cool, dry place.
If refrigerated, keep in a
tightly closed glass container
to prevent odor from
permeating other foods.

To peel cloves of garlic easily,
firmly press the cloves with the
handle of a knife to break the skin.

SIMPLE PATIO SUPPERS

*O*n a soft summer night, dining on a candle-lit patio or porch can add a touch of elegance to this simple meal. The Maple-Glazed Pork Chops can be prepared on the grill while the Savory New Potatoes with Chive Butter and Orange Peas Amandine are being cooked inside. Add a freshly tossed green salad and top off the meal with a sumptuous dessert, Grands! Biscuits Strawberry Shortcakes.

MAPLE-GLAZED PORK CHOPS

Yield: 4 servings   Prep Time: 35 minutes

CHOPS
- 4 pork chops (¾ inch thick)
- ¼ teaspoon salt
- ¼ teaspoon coarse ground black pepper

MAPLE GLAZE
- ¾ cup pure maple syrup or Hungry Jack® Microwave Ready Regular Syrup
- 2 tablespoons brown sugar
- 2 tablespoons ketchup
- 2 tablespoons prepared mustard
- 1 tablespoon Worcestershire sauce

GRILLING DIRECTIONS:
1. Heat grill. Rub both sides of pork chops with salt and pepper. In small saucepan, combine all glaze ingredients; mix well. Bring to a boil, stirring constantly. Set aside.

2. When ready to grill, place pork chops on gas grill over medium heat or on charcoal grill 4 to 6 inches from medium coals. Cook 15 minutes, turning once.

3. Brush pork chops with glaze. Cook an additional 10 minutes or until pork chops are no longer pink in center, turning once and brushing frequently with glaze. Bring any remaining glaze to a boil; serve with pork chops.

BROILING DIRECTIONS:
1. Prepare pork chops and glaze as directed above. Place pork chops on broiler pan.

2. Broil 4 to 6 inches from heat for 10 minutes, turning once.

3. Brush pork chops with glaze. Broil an additional 6 to 8 minutes or until pork chops are no longer pink in center, turning once and brushing frequently with glaze. Bring any remaining glaze to a boil; serve with pork chops.

SAVORY NEW POTATOES WITH CHIVE BUTTER

Yield: 4 (1-cup) servings
Prep Time: 15 minutes

- 10 small new red potatoes, quartered
- 3 tablespoons butter
- 2 tablespoons chopped fresh summer savory or 2 teaspoons dried summer savory leaves
- 2 tablespoons chopped fresh chives

1. Place potatoes in medium saucepan; add just enough water to cover. Cook over medium-high heat for 8 to 10 minutes or just until tender. Drain; return potatoes to saucepan.

2. Stir in all remaining ingredients. Cook over medium heat for 1 to 2 minutes or until butter is melted and flavors are blended, stirring occasionally.

Fresh herbs and herb combinations can add special flavor highlights. Summer savory has a warm, aromatic peppery flavor that makes it a favorite blending herb. Use the thin green leaves of this annual herb. Chives are the mildest member of the onion family. The dark green, tubular leaves are best used fresh.

GRANDS!® BISCUITS STRAWBERRY SHORTCAKES

Yield: 8 servings   Prep Time: 15 minutes (Ready in 35 minutes)

1 (17.3-oz.) can Pillsbury Grands!® Refrigerated Buttermilk Biscuits
2 tablespoons butter, melted
4 to 5 tablespoons sugar
1 cup whipping cream

2 tablespoons powdered sugar
¼ teaspoon vanilla
2 pints (4 cups) strawberries, sliced
2 pints (4 cups) blueberries

1. Heat oven to 375°F. Separate dough into 8 biscuits. Dip top and sides only of each biscuit in butter, then in sugar. Place, sugar side up, 2 inches apart on ungreased cookie sheet. Bake at 375°F for 13 to 17 minutes or until golden brown. Cool slightly.

2. In small bowl, beat whipping cream until soft peaks form. Gradually add powdered sugar and vanilla, beating until stiff peaks form.

3. To serve, split biscuits; place on 8 dessert plates. Layer biscuit with strawberries, blueberries and whipped cream. Serve immediately.

ORANGE PEAS AMANDINE

Yield: 4 servings Prep Time: 10 minutes

1 tablespoon butter
2 tablespoons orange marmalade

1 (15-oz.) can LeSueur® Very Young Small Early Peas or Green Giant® Sweet Peas, drained
⅓ cup sliced almonds, toasted*

1. Melt butter in medium saucepan. Add orange marmalade; stir until blended.

2. Gently stir in peas and almonds; cook until thoroughly heated.

TIP:
* To toast almonds, heat oven to 350°F. Spread in single layer on cookie sheet. Bake at 350°F for 5 to 7 minutes or until light golden brown.

AUTUMN DINNER

Choose any of these hearty and delicious recipes for a memorable Autumn dinner.

SAUDER HERITAGE INN

Archbold, Ohio

The Sauder Heritage Inn at the Sauder Village is located in Archbold, Ohio. Built among the picturesque farm fields of Northwest Ohio, guests will find an oasis of serenity and history.

The Sauder Heritage Inn, which opened in the fall of 1994, combines the amenities of a contemporary hotel with the ambiance of a country inn. The majestic, two-story timber-framed lobby is enhanced by hand-forged wrought-iron railings and hanging lamps crafted by the village blacksmith.

The warm glow of natural wood and the comfortable furnishings reflect an atmosphere of true country ambiance. The inn features 33 spacious rooms appointed with all the amenities found in a big city hotel.

Photo by Ron Forth

From mid-April through October, the Sauder Farm and Craft Village, adjacent to the Inn, offers visitors a look into rural 19th century living. There, in 34 carefully restored structures, costumed interpreters and internationally-respected craftsmen tell of the struggles and triumphs in the lives of the area's early settlers.

Fine food made from the freshest ingredients is a hallmark at Sauder's. The executive chef creates an array of delectable meals and desserts daily.

At the Sauder Heritage Inn, guests are able to experience a living history in the heartland of America.

CORN CUSTARD

Yield: 6 servings   Prep Time: 20 minutes (Ready in 50 minutes)

1   cup chicken broth
1   cup frozen or canned corn
4   eggs
¼   cup heavy cream
⅛   teaspoon pepper

6   slices bacon, cooked, crumbled
¼   cup (1 ounce) finely shredded
     Cheddar cheese
     butter to line cups

1. Heat oven to 350°F. Butter six 4-oz. custard cups. In small saucepan, bring broth to a boil. Add corn; return to a boil. Stir; reduce heat. Cover; simmer 3 to 5 minutes or until corn is tender. Cool slightly. Puree mixture in food processor until smooth.

2. In medium bowl, combine eggs and cream; beat until well blended. Stir in corn mixture and pepper.

3. Sprinkle bacon and cheese evenly into buttered custard cups. Pour egg mixture evenly into cups.

4. Bake at 350°F for 25 to 30 minutes or until knife inserted in center comes out clean. Run knife around edges of cups; turn out onto serving platter. Serve immediately.

WOODLAND MUSHROOM CHICKEN WITH SAUCE

Yield: 6 servings (1½ cups sauce)
Prep Time: 55 minutes
(Ready in 1 hour, 10 minutes)

STUFFING

1   pound fresh mushrooms
¼   cup (½ stick) butter
2   garlic cloves, minced
¼   cup cooking sherry
⅛   teaspoon salt
⅛   teaspoon pepper

CHICKEN

6   (6 to 7-ounce) skin-on boneless chicken breast halves
6   slices bacon
    Paprika

SAUCE

1   tablespoon butter
1½   cups chopped fresh mushrooms
2   green onions, sliced
¼   cup cooking sherry
1½   cups heavy cream
¼   teaspoon salt
⅛   teaspoon pepper

1. Heat oven to 350°F. Line 15x10x1-inch baking pan with foil; butter lightly. To make stuffing, place mushrooms in food processor bowl with metal blade; process until finely chopped.

2. In medium saucepan or skillet, melt butter over medium-high heat. Add garlic and mushrooms; cook about 20 minutes or until most of liquid has evaporated, stirring occasionally.

3. Stir in sherry, salt and pepper. Cook an additional 5 to 10 minutes or until mixture is dry and all of liquid has evaporated, stirring occasionally. Set stuffing aside to cool.

4. To prepare chicken, place chicken breast halves, skin side down, on cutting board; trim excess fat and skin. Place 2 heaping tablespoons cooled stuffing on center of each breast. Fold in all sides of each breast; turn over, skin side up. Wrap each chicken breast with bacon slice; secure ends with toothpicks. Sprinkle breasts with paprika; place in buttered pan.

5. Bake at 350°F for 30 to 35 minutes or until chicken is fork-tender and juices run clear.

6. Meanwhile, to prepare sauce, melt butter in large skillet over medium-high heat. Add chopped mushrooms and green onions; cook 3 minutes. Add sherry; cook an additional 5 to 8 minutes or until liquid is reduced by half. Add cream; cook about 10 minutes, stirring frequently, until thickened. Stir in salt and pepper. Serve sauce with chicken.

SQUASH SOUFFLÉ

Yield: 6 servings   Prep Time: 30 minutes
(Ready in 3 hours)

SOUFFLÉ

2   medium butternut squash (1 pound each)
4   tablespoons butter
½   cup firmly packed brown sugar
3   eggs
½   cup heavy cream
1   teaspoon salt
1   teaspoon cinnamon
½   teaspoon nutmeg

TOPPING

½   cup firmly packed brown sugar
½   cup chopped walnuts
1   tablespoon butter, softened

1. Heat oven to 350°F. Cut each squash in half; remove seeds. Place on ungreased cookie sheet. Fill each squash cavity with 1 tablespoon butter and 2 tablespoons brown sugar.

2. Bake at 350°F for 1 to 1½ hours; cool.

3. Butter 1½-quart casserole. Scoop squash from skins; place in large bowl. Beat squash until smooth. Add eggs and cream, salt, cinnamon and nutmeg; mix well. Spoon mixture into buttered casserole.

4. In small bowl, combine all topping ingredients; mix well. Sprinkle over top of squash mixture.

5. Bake at 350°F for 45 to 60 minutes or until mixture is set.

Do not wash mushrooms until ready for use. Dry thoroughly.

Fresh mushrooms will keep for up to 5 days if stored in a moisture-proof container.

PUMPKIN SWIRL CHEESECAKE

Yield: 8 servings   Prep Time: 40 minutes (Ready in 2 hours, 55 minutes)

CRUST

3   tablespoons butter, melted

1   cup crushed gingersnaps
      (about 25 cookies)

FILLING

4   (8-ounce) packages cream
      cheese, softened

1   cup sugar

3   tablespoons cornstarch

1   cup sour cream

¼   teaspoon salt

2   teaspoons vanilla

3   eggs

1   teaspoon lemon juice

¾   cup canned pumpkin

3   tablespoons brown sugar

2   tablespoons molasses

1   teaspoon cinnamon

¾   teaspoon ginger

½   teaspoon nutmeg

⅛   teaspoon cloves

1. Heat oven to 350°F. In small bowl, combine butter and cookie crumbs; mix well. Press in bottom of 9-inch springform pan.

2. In large bowl, beat cream cheese, sugar and 2 tablespoons of the cornstarch until smooth. Add sour cream, salt and vanilla; mix well. Add eggs 1 at a time, beating well after each addition.

3. Place 3½ cups batter in medium bowl; add lemon juice. Mix thoroughly; set aside.

4. To remaining batter in large bowl, add 1 tablespoon cornstarch and all remaining ingredients; beat well. Set aside 1 cup of the pumpkin batter.

5. Pour half of vanilla batter (1¾ cups) into crust. Top with 2 cups pumpkin batter, remaining half of vanilla batter and reserved 1 cup pumpkin batter. Swirl batters with knife or spoon.

6. Bake at 350°F for 1 to 1¼ hours or until filling is almost set in center. Cool in pan on wire rack for 1 hour. Run knife around edge of pan. Remove sides of pan. Serve warm or refrigerate until serving time.

AFTER SCHOOL SNACKS

*T*his selection of recipes for after school snacks offers great versatility. Corn Dog Twists are quick to make to satisfy hearty appetites. Chocolate Peanut Butter Dip stirs together in just minutes for a sweet treat. Fruit and Yogurtsicles can be on hand in the freezer for a cool, refreshing snack. Making the Cookie Pops can be a delightful after school activity. They can be enjoyed with a glass of milk as soon as they are completed or enjoyed later as the family meal dessert.

COOKIE POPS

Yield: 12 cookie pops
Prep Time: 45 minutes

1   (18-oz.) pkg.
    Pillsbury
    Refrigerated Cookies
    with M&M's®
    Candies
18 flat wooden sticks
    with round ends

1   (6-oz.) pkg.
    (1 cup) semi-sweet
    chocolate chips
1   tablespoon
    butter

1. Heat oven to 350°F. Shape tablespoonfuls of well-chilled dough into 12 (1½-inch) balls. Arrange in circle on ungreased cookie sheets, 3 inches apart and 2 inches from edges; flatten slightly. Securely insert wooden stick into each cookie with end pointing toward center of cookie sheet.

2. Bake at 350°F for 8 to 11 minutes or until lightly browned around edges. Cool 2 minutes; remove from cookie sheet. Cool 15 minutes or until completely cooled.

3. In small saucepan, melt chips and butter over low heat, stirring constantly. Dip half of cookie into chocolate. Place on waxed paper until chocolate is firm. Garnish as desired.

TIP:
For peanut butter dip, substitute 1 cup peanut butter chips for chocolate chips.

CHOCOLATE PEANUT BUTTER DIP

Yield: 10 servings
Prep Time: 5 minutes

¾ cup Pillsbury Creamy
    Supreme® Chocolate
    Fudge Frosting
½ cup peanut butter

¼ cup milk
3⅓ cups animal or teddy
    bear crackers

In medium bowl, combine all ingredients except crackers; mix well. Serve as dip with crackers.

To make preparation of Chocolate Peanut Butter Dip easier if you store frosting and peanut butter in the refrigerator, place ingredients in a microwave-safe bowl and microwave on HIGH for 5 seconds or until frosting and peanut butter are softened.

Corn Dog Twists

Yield: 8 sandwiches   Prep Time: 5 minutes (Ready in 30 minutes)

1   (11.5-oz.) can Pillsbury Refrigerated
    Cornbread Twists
8   hot dogs

1   tablespoon butter, melted
1   tablespoon grated Parmesan cheese

1. Heat oven to 375°F. Unroll dough into 1 long sheet. Seal crosswise center perforations. Separate dough into 8 long strips (2 cornbread twists each). Wrap 1 strip around each hot dog; place on ungreased cookie sheet with ends of dough tucked under hot dog. Brush each with butter; sprinkle with cheese.

2. Bake at 375°F for 12 to 16 minutes or until light golden brown. Remove from cookie sheet; serve immediately.

Fruit and Yogurtsicles

Yield: 8 pops   Prep Time: 20 minutes (Ready in 6 hours, 20 minutes)

3   small ripe bananas, cut into chunks
1   (6-oz.) can frozen orange juice
    concentrate
2   (8-oz.) containers low-fat
    vanilla yogurt

8   (5-oz.) paper drink cups
8   flat wooden sticks with round ends

1. In blender container, combine bananas and orange juice concentrate. Cover; blend until smooth. Add yogurt. Cover; blend until smooth. Pour into paper drink cups, filling about ¾ full.

2. Cover each cup with foil. Make small hole in center of foil; insert wooden stick through hole and yogurt mixture to bottom of cup. Freeze at least 6 hours or until firm. To serve, remove foil and gently push from bottom of cup to release pops.

FAVORITES FROM THE HEARTLAND

A classic selection of recipes from the Midwest.

WINDMILL INN
Chapman, Kansas

Windmill Inn, located near Abilene, Kansas, is a Prairie Style Four Square home built in 1917 by the innkeeper's grandfather, Henry Delker.

In 1991, the home was transformed into a bed and breakfast inn, recreating the charm of a bygone era. Special attention has been given to every detail of the restoration. The wraparound front porch lures you to come enjoy the sights and sounds of country life, while relaxing in a porch swing or rocking chair.

The Windmill Inn has four guest rooms, each with its own distinctive and charming decor.

In the morning, guests awaken to the aroma of the full country breakfast being prepared in the kitchen.

After a day's tour of historic Abilene, guests may return to the Inn for an evening meal that will complete their perfect day.

The hospitality and accommodations found at the Windmill Inn reflect the quality and comfort desired by even the most sophisticated traveler.

FRENCH TOAST WITH ORANGE SYRUP

Yield: 4 servings Prep Time: 30 minutes

ORANGE SYRUP
- ⅓ cup firmly packed brown sugar
- ¼ cup frozen orange juice concentrate
- 1 tablespoon water
- ¼ cup (½ stick) butter, softened
- ¼ cup honey
- 1 tablespoon maple syrup
- 1 to 2 teaspoons grated orange peel

FRENCH TOAST
- 2 eggs
- ½ cup milk
- ¼ teaspoon nutmeg
- 1½ cups crushed corn flakes cereal
- 8 (¾ to 1-inch thick) slices day-old French bread
- 2 tablespoons to ¼ cup (½ stick) butter
- 2 tablespoons sugar

1. In small saucepan, bring brown sugar, orange juice concentrate and water to a boil. Meanwhile, in blender container or food processor fitted with metal blade, combine butter, honey, maple syrup and orange peel; blend until smooth. With machine running, pour hot orange mixture into the butter mixture, mixing until well blended; set aside.

2. In shallow bowl, combine eggs, milk and nutmeg; beat until well blended. In shallow pan, place crushed cereal. Quickly dip both sides of bread in egg mixture; coat with cereal.

3. Melt 2 tablespoons butter in large skillet over medium-high heat. Add coated slices of bread; cook about 1 to 2 minutes on each side or until golden brown. Sprinkle with sugar. Serve warm with orange syrup.

STEAK WITH HERBED BUTTER

Yield: 4 servings (½ cup herbed butter)   Prep Time: 25 minutes

HERBED BUTTER

½   *cup (1 stick) unsalted butter, softened*

1   *teaspoon seasoned salt*

½   *teaspoon dried thyme leaves, crushed*

½   *teaspoon dried oregano leaves, crushed*

¼   *teaspoon freshly ground black pepper*

3   *tablespoons chopped fresh parsley*

STEAK

1½   *pounds beef tenderloin steak (filet mignon)*

1. In small bowl, combine all herbed butter ingredients; blend well.

2. Broil or grill steak to desired doneness. Remove from pan or grill; cut steak into thin slices. Serve steak slices topped with herbed butter.

CRANBERRY PECAN COFFEE CAKE

Yield: 10 to 12 servings   Prep Time: 20 minutes
(Ready in 1 hour, 20 minutes)

TOPPING
- ¾ cup chopped pecans
- 4 teaspoons sugar
- ½ teaspoon cinnamon

BATTER
- 2 cups all-purpose flour
- 1 teaspoon baking powder
- 1 teaspoon baking soda
- ½ teaspoon salt
- 1½ teaspoons almond extract
- 1 cup sour cream
- 1 cup sugar
- ½ cup (1 stick) butter, softened
- 2 eggs
- 1 (16-ounce) can whole berry cranberry sauce

1. Heat oven to 350°F. Butter 10-inch tube pan. In small bowl, combine all topping ingredients; mix well. Spoon mixture in bottom of buttered pan.

2. In medium bowl, combine flour, baking powder, baking soda and salt; mix well. In small bowl, combine almond extract and sour cream.

3. In large bowl, beat sugar and butter until fluffy. Add eggs one at a time, beating well after each addition. Add flour mixture alternately with sour cream mixture, mixing well. Pour ¾ of batter (about 3 cups) over topping mixture in pan. Carefully spread cranberry sauce over batter. Spoon remaining batter over cranberry sauce; spread evenly.

4. Bake at 350°F for 45 to 55 minutes or until toothpick inserted in center comes out clean. Cool in pan 15 minutes. Run knife around edges and bottom to loosen; invert onto serving plate. Serve warm.

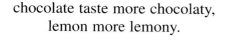

The Secret to Bringing Out Flavors
Butter is many a chef's secret for bringing out the best in his or her creations, and here's why: Not only does the butter lend its own unmistakable flavor to foods, it also enhances other flavors. For example, butter makes chocolate taste more chocolaty, lemon more lemony.

Baking with Butter
To evenly distribute spices and flavorings in a batter, cream them with butter.

•

Baked goods made with butter generally stay fresh and moist longer.

If a recipe calls for preheating the oven, allow 10 to 15 minutes for it to reach the proper temperature.

COUNTRY CASSEROLES

*T*hese casserole recipes offer old-fashioned goodness with new-fashioned ease.
The convenience of frozen vegetables, a prepared sauce and
refrigerated biscuits make Big Country Garden Casserole a snap to make.
Casserole from a slow cooker? Try Cheesy Ham Au Gratin.
No lengthy preparation for Classic Chicken Pot Pie or Green Bean and
Turkey Casserole - just warm and hearty meals perfect
when the autumn leaves are falling.

BIG COUNTRY® GARDEN CASSEROLE

Yield: 6 servings   Prep Time: 15 minutes
(Ready in 40 minutes)

1¼ lb. ground turkey
1 (1-lb.) pkg. Green Giant Select® Frozen Broccoli, Carrots and Cauliflower, thawed
1 (14.5-oz.) jar Alfredo sauce

½ teaspoon dried basil leaves
1 (12-oz.) can Pillsbury Big Country® Refrigerated Buttermilk Biscuits
1 tablespoon grated Parmesan cheese

1. Heat oven to 375°F. In large skillet, brown ground turkey. Add vegetables, Alfredo sauce and basil; mix well. Cook and stir over medium-high heat until mixture boils. Reduce heat; cook and stir 4 minutes or until thoroughly heated.

2. Separate dough into 10 biscuits. Cut two ½-inch deep slashes crosswise in top of each biscuit with knife to form an X. Pour hot turkey mixture into ungreased 12x8-inch (2-quart) baking dish. Arrange biscuits in 2 rows of 5 biscuits each on top of hot mixture. Sprinkle with cheese.

3. Bake at 375°F for 16 to 22 minutes or until biscuits are deep golden brown.

CHEESY HAM AU GRATIN

Yield: 4 (1¾-cup) servings   Prep Time: 10 minutes
(Ready in 8 hours, 10 minutes)

2   cups diced cooked ham
2   cups milk
1   cup boiling water
2   (11-oz.) cans Green Giant® Mexicorn® Whole Kernel Corn, Red and Green Peppers, drained
1   (10¾-oz.) can condensed Cheddar cheese soup
1   (7.8-oz.) pkg. Hungry Jack® Cheesy Scalloped Potatoes

1. In 3½ or 4-quart slow cooker, combine all ingredients; mix well, making sure potato slices are covered with sauce.

2. Cover; cook on low setting for at least 8 hours or until potatoes are tender.

GREEN BEAN AND TURKEY CASSEROLE

Yield: 6 servings   Prep Time: 35 minutes

1½   to 2 cups cubed cooked turkey or chicken
1   (14.5-oz.) can Green Giant® Cut Green Beans, drained
1   (10¾-oz.) can condensed cream of mushroom soup
⅓   cup milk
4   oz. (1 cup) shredded Cheddar cheese
6   servings Hungry Jack® Mashed Potatoes (prepared as directed on package)
½   (2.8-oz.) can french fried onions

1. Heat oven to 375°F. In medium saucepan, combine turkey, green beans, soup and milk; mix well. Cook over medium heat until mixture is hot, stirring occasionally.

2. Remove saucepan from heat. Add cheese; stir until melted. Pour into ungreased 2-quart casserole. Top with prepared mashed potatoes.

3. Bake at 375°F for 10 minutes. Sprinkle with onions; bake an additional 3 to 5 minutes or until mixture is bubbly and onions are warm.

CLASSIC CHICKEN POT PIE

Yield: 6 servings   Prep Time: 20 minutes
(Ready in 1 hour)

1   (15-oz.) pkg. Pillsbury Refrigerated Pie Crusts
⅓   cup butter
⅓   cup Pillsbury BEST® All Purpose Flour
⅓   cup chopped onion
¾   teaspoon salt
¼   teaspoon pepper
1½   cups chicken broth
⅔   cup milk
2½   to 3 cups cubed cooked chicken or turkey
2   cups Green Giant® Frozen Mixed Vegetables, thawed

1. Heat oven to 425°F. Prepare pie crusts as directed on package for *two-crust* pie using 9-inch pie pan.

2. In medium saucepan, melt butter over medium heat. Add onion; cook about 2 minutes or until tender. Stir in flour, onion, salt and pepper until well blended, stirring constantly. Gradually stir in broth and milk; cook, stirring constantly, until bubbly and thickened.

3. Add chicken and vegetables; mix well. Spoon chicken filling into crust-lined pan. Top with second crust and flute; cut slits in several places.

4. Bake 425°F for 28 to 38 minutes or until crust is golden brown.

When a recipe calls for cubed, cooked chicken, you can plan for one 3 to 4-lb. fryer to yield 3 to 4 cups and two whole chicken breasts (1½ lbs. with skin and bone) or ¾ lb. chicken breast (skinned and boned) to yield about 2 cups.

COUNTRY INN SPECIALITIES

Add a dash of country inn charm to your recipe file with these country inn specialities.

WHITE LACE INN

Sturgeon Bay, Wisconsin

*T*he White Lace Inn is located in the picturesque town of Sturgeon Bay, Wisconsin. Built as a private home in 1903, it has been operating as a Victorian country inn since 1982.

This classic country-style bed and breakfast neighborhood features 18 charming guest rooms in four Victorian homes. Some guest rooms have canopy beds, whirlpools and fireplaces. In any case, all the rooms offer the utmost in comfort and charm.

The homespun atmosphere found at the White Lace Inn starts with its porch filled with white wicker furniture and carries through into its main parlor where guests can enjoy lemonade, a cookie jar filled with delicious homemade cookies, a fireplace where guests can gather to play parlor games, read or relax with a bowl of freshly popped popcorn.

Guests can always look forward to fabulous breakfasts at the White Lace Inn. Every breakfast offers a hot main dish, assorted fresh baked muffins, as well as their house specialty - Scandinavian fruit soups.

The White Lace Inn is known as a haven specializing in personal service for those seeking relaxation and country charm.

CHERRY-APPLE BREAKFAST CRISP

Yield: 12 servings   Prep Time: 50 minutes (Ready in 1 hour, 20 minutes)

10 cups sliced peeled apples (such as McIntosh)	1 cup firmly packed brown sugar
2 cups frozen sweet cherries, thawed, drained	⅔ cup all-purpose flour
	⅔ cup butter, softened
2 cups old-fashioned rolled oats	2 teaspoons cinnamon
	1 teaspoon nutmeg

1. Heat oven to 375°F. Butter 13x9-inch (3-quart) baking dish. Arrange apples and cherries in buttered baking dish.

2. In medium bowl, combine oats, brown sugar, flour, butter, cinnamon and nutmeg; mix well. Sprinkle over apples and cherries.

3. Bake at 375°F for 30 to 35 minutes or until apples are tender. Serve warm.

OATMEAL CHOCOLATE-TOFFEE COOKIES

Yield: 2 dozen cookies   Prep Time: 25 minutes
(Ready in 45 minutes)

1 cup sugar	*1 teaspoon baking soda*
1 cup firmly packed brown sugar	*3½ cups old-fashioned rolled oats*
1 cup (2 sticks) butter, softened	*½ (7-ounce) milk chocolate candy bar, chopped*
2 teaspoons vanilla	
2 eggs	*3 (1.4-ounce) toffee candy bars, chopped*
2¼ cups all-purpose flour	*½ cup chopped nuts, if desired*
1 teaspoon baking powder	

1. Heat oven to 375°F. In large bowl, beat sugar, brown sugar and butter until light and fluffy. Add vanilla and eggs; beat well.

2. In medium bowl, combine flour, baking powder and baking soda; mix well. Add to butter mixture; mix until well combined. Stir in rolled oats, candy and nuts. Drop by tablespoonfuls onto unbuttered cookie sheets.

3. Bake at 375°F for 8 to 10 minutes. (Centers will look slightly underbaked.)

For best results when baking, bring all ingredients to room temperature.

Buttering Pans

Buttering baking pans and cookie sheets is necessary only when recipes specify to do so. To butter a pan, spread a thin, even layer of butter over a cookie sheet, inside muffin cups and cake pans, or over the bottom and ½ inch up the sides of a loaf pan. Use a paper towel or the butter wrapper for easy spreading. Do not use the butter called for in the ingredient list for buttering pans.

Evenly space cookies on a cookie sheet for uniform baking.

Always place dough on cooled cookie sheets; otherwise, the dough will spread before it's in the oven, resulting in improperly baked and irregularly shaped cookies.

CRUNCHY APPLE-CRANBERRY MUFFINS

Yield: 18 muffins   Prep Time: 25 minutes (Ready in 45 minutes)

1½	cups all-purpose flour		1	cup milk
3	teaspoons baking powder		¼	cup sour cream
1	teaspoon cinnamon		2	eggs
1	cup old-fashioned rolled oats		1	cup chopped peeled apples
½	cup firmly packed brown sugar		½	cup halved fresh or frozen cranberries
¼	cup (½ stick) butter, melted		2	tablespoons sugar

1. Heat oven to 425°F. Butter 18 muffin cups. In large bowl, combine flour, baking powder and cinnamon; mix well. Stir in rolled oats and brown sugar.

2. In medium bowl, beat butter, milk, sour cream and eggs until well blended. Add to dry ingredients; mix just until dry ingredients are moistened. Stir in apples and cranberries. Fill buttered muffin cups ¾ full. Sprinkle sugar evenly over muffins.

3. Bake at 425°F for 15 to 20 minutes or until light golden brown.

TIP:
If desired, chopped fresh rhubarb and cherries can be substituted for the apples and cranberries.

HALLOWEEN PARTY

*H*alloween is a magic night for kids, and what better way for the little goblins to have fun than to have a neighborhood costume party? Monster Dilly Dip makes eating some fresh veggies fun and tasty. To carry out the Halloween theme, select orange and green vegetables that kids enjoy. Chicken Fingers and Butter Crumb Breadsticks are quick to prepare and easy to eat. Crazy Cookie Creatures will also help set the stage for the party, serving as a centerpiece at the beginning, and later, for snacking.

BUTTER CRUMB BREADSTICKS

Yield: 16 breadsticks   Prep Time: 10 minutes
(Ready in 25 minutes)

10	buttery round crackers, crushed	1	(11-oz.) can Pillsbury Refrigerated Breadsticks
1	tablespoon grated Parmesan cheese	1	tablespoon butter, melted
1	teaspoon dried parsley flakes		

1. Heat oven to 350°F. In small bowl, combine crushed crackers, Parmesan cheese and parsley flakes; mix well.

2. Unroll dough; separate at perforations to form 8 strips. Cut each strip in half crosswise; twist on flat surface. Place 1 inch apart on 1 large or 2 small ungreased cookie sheets. Press ends down firmly on cookie sheet. Brush each breadstick with butter; sprinkle evenly with cracker mixture.

3. Bake at 350°F for 14 to 16 minutes or until golden brown. Serve warm.

CHICKEN FINGERS

Yield: 30 chicken fingers   Prep Time: 10 minutes
(Ready in 25 minutes)

1	egg	1	cup Progresso® Italian Style Bread Crumbs*
1	lb. boneless skinless chicken breast halves or thighs, cut into ½-inch strips		Progresso® Marinara Sauce

1. Heat oven to 375°F. In small bowl, beat egg slightly. Dip chicken strips in egg; roll in bread crumbs, coating evenly. Place on ungreased cookie sheet.

2. Bake at 375°F for 10 to 15 minutes or until chicken is no longer pink and coating is crisp. Serve with marinara sauce.

TIP:
* Progresso® Garlic and Herb or Parmesan Bread Crumbs can be substituted for the Italian Style Bread Crumbs.

MONSTER DILLY DIP

Yield: 2 cups   Prep Time: 10 minutes
(Ready in 2 hours, 10 minutes)

1½	cups sour cream	2	tablespoons dried dill weed
⅔	cup mayonnaise	1	teaspoon celery salt or seasoned salt
2	tablespoons instant minced onion	4	drops green food color
2	tablespoons dried parsley flakes		

1. In small bowl, combine all ingredients; mix well. Cover; refrigerate at least 2 hours to blend flavors.

2. Serve with cut-up fresh green and orange vegetables.

CRAZY COOKIE CREATURES

Yield: 18 cookies   Prep Time: 10 minutes (Ready in 20 minutes)

1   (18-oz.) pkg. Pillsbury Refrigerated
    Sugar Cookies

¼   cup sugar

4   rolls fruit flavored, ring-shaped
    hard candies
    Candy corn

FROSTING*

1   cup powdered sugar

1   tablespoon milk

1   tablespoon butter, softened
    Food color

1. Heat oven to 350°F. Line cookie sheets with foil. Cut cookie dough into 18 (½-inch) slices. Shape each into ball, roll in sugar. Place 4 inches apart on foil-lined cookie sheets. Flatten into 4-inch circles, dipping fingers in sugar if necessary to prevent sticking. Firmly press ring-shaped candies in dough for eyes. Press candy corn in dough for ears, horns, teeth, beak or mouth to create desired creature. (Candies must be placed in dough, without extending beyond edge of dough.)

2. Bake at 350°F for 8 to 10 minutes or until edges are golden brown. Cool completely; remove from foil.

3. In small bowl, combine powdered sugar, milk and butter; blend until smooth. If necessary, add additional milk one drop at a time for desired piping consistency. Add food color as desired. Using decorating bag or knife, decorate cookies as desired.

TIP:
*Pillsbury Creamy Supreme® Frosting can be substituted for the frosting.

DAIRY DELIGHTS

Add that special taste of wholesome goodness to your recipes by including dairy products.

KINGSLEY INN
Fort Madison, Iowa

*T*he elegant Kingsley Inn is located in Fort Madison, Iowa.

Overlooking the Mississippi River, the Inn was originally built in 1860 as a brick and wood commercial property. In 1990, the building was painstakingly converted into a small luxury inn, reflecting the aura of another age…one of Victorian elegance and grace.

Decorated in the style of the 19th century, each of the 14 rooms are filled with exquisitely restored antiques, beautiful draperies and wall coverings. Tasteful attention to detail, combined with all the luxurious amenities of

today, creates a memorable experience for each guest.

Breakfast at the Kingsley Inn is served in the gracious morning room. The Victorian-style room is richly decorated with floral carpeting, mahogany sideboard, and carved rosewood chairs. Home baked pastries, fresh fruit and breads are served on tables set with the finest china, beautiful linens, silver and crystal.

Your stay at the Kingsley Inn will enchant you with the aura of another age, a period when life was slower, more peaceful; when courteous people took the time to care.

LEMON BREAD

Yield: 12 slices   Prep Time: 15 minutes (Ready in 1 hour, 15 minutes)

BREAD
- 1   cup sugar
- 1/3   cup (2/3 stick) butter, softened
- 1/2   teaspoon lemon extract
- 2   eggs
- 2   cups flour

- 1   teaspoon baking powder
- 3/4   teaspoon salt
- 1/2   teaspoon baking soda
- 1/2   cup buttermilk or milk
- 2   teaspoons grated lemon rind
- 3/4   cup chopped walnuts

GLAZE
- 2   tablespoons sugar
- 2   tablespoons fresh lemon juice

1. Heat oven to 350°F. Butter and flour bottom only of an 8x4 or 9x5-inch loaf pan.

2. In medium bowl, combine sugar, butter and lemon extract; beat until light and fluffy. Add eggs, one at a time, beating after each addition.

3. In small bowl, combine flour, baking powder, salt and baking soda; blend well. Add alternately with buttermilk to sugar mixture, blending well after each addition. Stir in lemon rind and walnuts.

4. Bake at 350°F for 50 to 60 minutes or until toothpick inserted in center comes out clean. Cool loaf 5 minutes; remove from pan.

5. Combine glaze ingredients in small saucepan; bring to a boil to dissolve sugar. Brush glaze over top of warm loaf.

GOOEY BUTTER CAKE

Yield: 12 servings   Prep Time: 25 minutes (Ready in 1 hour)

CRUST

1   *(1 pound 2.5-ounce)*
    package yellow
    cake mix

½   *cup (1 stick)*
    butter, softened

1   *egg, beaten*

FILLING

1   *(8-ounce) package*
    cream cheese,
    softened

2   *cups powdered sugar*

1   *teaspoon vanilla*

2   *eggs*

TOPPING

1½ *cups cherry pie filling,*
    if desired

1. Heat oven to 350°F. Butter 13x9-inch pan. In large bowl, combine cake mix, butter and 1 egg; mix until well combined. Press in bottom of buttered pan.

2. In small bowl, combine cream cheese, powdered sugar, vanilla and eggs; mix until smooth and creamy. Pour over crust.

3. Bake at 350°F for 30 to 35 minutes or until lightly browned. Serve warm or cool. Cut into squares; top with cherry pie filling.

CHEESE-FILLED COFFEE BREAD

Yield: 15 servings   Prep Time: 40 minutes
(Ready in 4 hours, 15 minutes)

BREAD

2   packages active dry yeast

¼   cup warm water

2½   cups all-purpose flour

1   tablespoon sugar

1   teaspoon salt

1   cup (2 sticks) butter

4   egg yolks

4   egg whites, slightly beaten

FILLING

2   (8-ounce) package cream cheese, softened

1   cup sugar

1   teaspoon lemon juice

1   egg yolk

TOPPING

1   egg white, slightly beaten

½   cup finely chopped nuts

GLAZE

1   cup powdered sugar

3   to 4 teaspoons milk or water

1. In small bowl, dissolve yeast in warm water (105° to 115°F). Let stand 5 minutes.

2. In large bowl, combine flour, 1 tablespoon sugar and salt; mix well. Cut in butter until coarse crumbs form. Add 4 egg yolks; mix well. Add yeast mixture; mix well. Add 4 egg whites; mix well. Cover; refrigerate 2 to 3 hours.

3. Meanwhile, in medium bowl, combine cream cheese, 1 cup sugar, lemon juice and 1 egg yolk; beat until smooth. Set aside. Lightly butter 15x10x1-inch baking pan.

4. Divide chilled dough in half. (Dough will be sticky.) Press half of the dough into buttered pan. Spread filling over dough.

5. On floured surface, roll remaining half of dough to 15x10-inch rectangle. Place dough over filling; seal edges. Brush top with beaten egg white; sprinkle with nuts. Cover loosely with buttered plastic wrap and cloth towel. Let rise in warm place (80° to 85°F.) for 1 hour.

6. Heat oven to 350°F. Uncover dough. Bake 25 to 30 minutes or until bread is light golden brown. Cool 5 minutes.

7. In small bowl, combine glaze ingredients; blend until smooth. Drizzle over bread. Cut into squares; serve warm.

Cream cheese can be softened in the microwave oven for ease in blending or spreading. Remove from foil package and place on a microwave-safe plate. Microwave 8 ounces of cream cheese on MEDIUM for 1 to 1½ minutes or just until softened (do not melt).

Eggs will separate best when cold from the refrigerator. To avoid getting a little yolk in a bowl of whites, separate each egg into a small bowl, then combine with other separated whites and yolks. To beat egg whites to highest volume, bring whites to room temperature and prevent the presence of any fat, which reduces foaming action. Make sure the whites contain no specks of yolk and that the beaters and bowl are free of any oil residue.

BUTTER BASICS

BUTTER VARIETIES

Lightly Salted Butter

Lightly salted butter is used as table butter and for general cooking. When creating flavored butters, lightly salted butter is best used in savory butters, such as those containing herbs or wine.

Unsalted Butter

Unsalted butter, also known as "sweet butter," has no salt added and has the rich, pure taste of sweet cream. It is best used for baking or when making sweet flavored butters.

Whipped Butter

Whipped butter contains more air and moisture than regular butter. It spreads more easily when chilled than regular butter and is generally used as a table spread. Because its weight and density is not the same as an equal measure of regular butter, it should not be used in recipes unless specified.

CREATING BUTTER SHAPES

Molded Butter

- To mold: Beat softened butter with electric mixer or by hand until smooth. Pack mold with butter, and refrigerate or freeze.
- To unmold: Dip the filled mold in a bowl of hot tap water. Run a sharp knife along the edge. Place a serving tray on top of mold; flip tray and mold over, so that molded butter is on the serving tray.

Butter Curls

Use a ¼-pound stick of butter that has been kept at room temperature for several minutes until it softens slightly but is still firm. Heat butter curler in very hot water, then pull lightly but firmly over the butter to form curls. If curls break, the butter is too cold. Reheat curler as necessary.

BUTTER STORAGE

Store butter refrigerated or frozen, well-wrapped or in a sealed container, and away from vegetables and other highly aromatic foods.

Refrigerated

- Unopened butter keeps in the refrigerator for several weeks.
- Store opened butter, covered, in the refrigerator butter keeper.

Frozen

- To freeze butter, seal in a plastic freezer bag or wrap tightly with heavy-duty foil.
- Butter may be frozen up to 9 months.
- For best flavor, store unsalted butter in the freezer until ready to use.

MAKING FLAVORED BUTTERS

Flavored or compound butter is a terrific way to add richness to chicken, fish, vegetables and breads. To make flavored butters, simply stir minced garlic, snipped herbs, spices, or nuts into softened butter. Form the mixture into a roll or small balls, wrap in plastic wrap, and refrigerate. Use the flavored butter anytime you need a special spread, topping, or garnish.

To give butter a wonderful nutty flavor, cook it until golden brown or the color of a copper penny. This browning gives butter a sweet taste that is excellent over vegetables, for caramel-type sauces, and in a butter frosting for a carrot or applesauce cake.

INDEX

(Continued on page 76)

INDEX

Seasonal Savings from Pillsbury

Seasonal Savings from Pillsbury

25¢

SAVE 25¢ On ONE Package of Pillsbury Crescent Rolls

53733

5 18000 07225 0 (8101)0 53733 1298

CONSUMER: Limit one coupon per purchase of specified product(s); no other coupon may be used with this coupon. Void if sold, exchanged, or transferred. **RETAILER:** You are authorized to act as our agent and redeem this coupon at face value plus 8¢ handling if in accordance with our redemption policy, copies available on request. Send coupons to THE PILLSBURY COMPANY, P.O. Box 23001, Nogales, AZ 85662. Void if copied. Void where prohibited, licensed or regulated. Good only in USA and APO/FPO post office addresses. Cash Value .001¢. ©1997 The Pillsbury Company

---

55¢/2

SAVE 55¢ When you purchase BOTH Pillsbury Moist Supreme® Cake Mix and Creamy Supreme® Frosting

50698

5 18000 40028 2 (8101)0 50698 1298

CONSUMER: Limit one coupon per purchase of specified product(s); no other coupon may be used with this coupon. Void if sold, exchanged, or transferred. **RETAILER:** You are authorized to act as our agent and redeem this coupon at face value plus 8¢ handling if in accordance with our redemption policy, copies available on request. Send coupons to THE PILLSBURY COMPANY, P.O. Box 23001, Nogales, AZ 85662. Void if copied. Void where prohibited, licensed or regulated. Good only in USA and APO/FPO post office addresses. Cash Value .001¢. ©1997 The Pillsbury Company

---

25¢

SAVE 25¢ On ONE Package of Pillsbury Quick Bread Mix

50699

5 18000 43425 6 (8101)0 50699 1298

CONSUMER: Limit one coupon per purchase of specified product(s); no other coupon may be used with this coupon. Void if sold, exchanged, or transferred. **RETAILER:** You are authorized to act as our agent and redeem this coupon at face value plus 8¢ handling if in accordance with our redemption policy, copies available on request. Send coupons to THE PILLSBURY COMPANY, P.O. Box 23001, Nogales, AZ 85662. Void if copied. Void where prohibited, licensed or regulated. Good only in USA and APO/FPO post office addresses. Cash Value .001¢. ©1997 The Pillsbury Company

---

30¢/2

SAVE 30¢ On TWO Packages of Pillsbury Grands!® Biscuits

53736

5 18000 15058 3 (8101)0 53736 1298

CONSUMER: Limit one coupon per purchase of specified product(s); no other coupon may be used with this coupon. Void if sold, exchanged, or transferred. **RETAILER:** You are authorized to act as our agent and redeem this coupon at face value plus 8¢ handling if in accordance with our redemption policy, copies available on request. Send coupons to THE PILLSBURY COMPANY, P.O. Box 23001, Nogales, AZ 85662. Void if copied. Void where prohibited, licensed or regulated. Good only in USA and APO/FPO post office addresses. Cash Value .001¢. ©1997 The Pillsbury Company

---

25¢

SAVE 25¢ On ONE Package of Pillsbury Grands!® Sweet Rolls

53738

5 18000 15025 5 (8101)0 53738 1298

CONSUMER: Limit one coupon per purchase of specified product(s); no other coupon may be used with this coupon. Void if sold, exchanged, or transferred. **RETAILER:** You are authorized to act as our agent and redeem this coupon at face value plus 8¢ handling if in accordance with our redemption policy, copies available on request. Send coupons to THE PILLSBURY COMPANY, P.O. Box 23001, Nogales, AZ 85662. Void if copied. Void where prohibited, licensed or regulated. Good only in USA and APO/FPO post office addresses. Cash Value .001¢. ©1997 The Pillsbury Company

---

25¢

SAVE 25¢ On ONE Package of Pillsbury Sweet Rolls

53737

5 18000 08125 2 (8101)0 53737 1298

CONSUMER: Limit one coupon per purchase of specified product(s); no other coupon may be used with this coupon. Void if sold, exchanged, or transferred. **RETAILER:** You are authorized to act as our agent and redeem this coupon at face value plus 8¢ handling if in accordance with our redemption policy, copies available on request. Send coupons to THE PILLSBURY COMPANY, P.O. Box 23001, Nogales, AZ 85662. Void if copied. Void where prohibited, licensed or regulated. Good only in USA and APO/FPO post office addresses. Cash Value .001¢. ©1997 The Pillsbury Company

SAVE 40¢ On THREE Packages of Big Country® Biscuits

SAVE 40¢ On THREE Packages of Hungry Jack® Biscuits

SAVE 25¢ On ONE Package of Pillsbury Garlic Breadsticks

SAVE 30¢ On ONE Old El Paso® Dinner Kit or Shells

SAVE 40¢ On ONE Old El Paso® Sauce or Dip

SAVE 25¢ On ONE Package of Pillsbury Dinner Breads

Special Offer – Order Today!

☑ **YES!** Please send me Pillsbury's *Best of the Bake-Off®* Cookbook for $19.95 (shipping and handling included).
***All orders must be pre-paid. U.S. orders only.**

Send this card along with check or money order payable to Pillsbury Publications to: Pillsbury Publications, Dept. 7006, P.O. Box 400863, Des Moines, IA 50340.

Name _____

Address _____

City _____

State _____ Zip _____

For Credit Card Orders Call: 1-800-611-1601

Item No: HBEST

*Offer good while quantities last. Please allow 6-8 weeks for delivery.

©1997 The Pillsbury Company